It's Greek to Me!

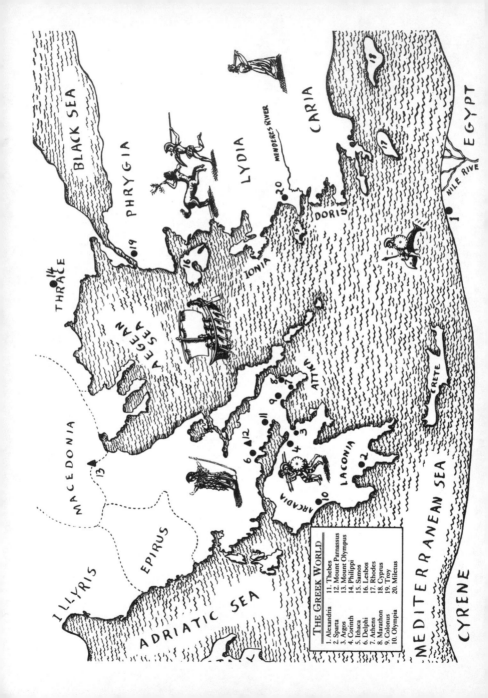

BLACK SEA

THRACE

PHRYGIA

LYDIA

CARIA

MENDERES RIVER

DORIS

EGYPT

NILE RIVER

MACEDONIA

AEGEAN SEA

IONIA

ILLYRIS

EPIRUS

ATTICA

LACONIA

ARCADIA

ADRIATIC SEA

MEDITERRANEAN SEA

CRETE

CYRENE

THE GREEK WORLD	
1. Alexandria	11. Thebes
2. Sparta	12. Mount Parnassus
3. Argos	13. Mount Olympus
4. Corinth	14. Philippi
5. Ithaca	15. Samos
6. Delphi	16. Lesbos
7. Athens	17. Rhodes
8. Marathon	18. Cyprus
9. Colonus	19. Troy
10. Olympia	20. Miletus

It's Greek to Me!

BRUSH UP YOUR CLASSICS

MICHAEL MACRONE
ILLUSTRATIONS BY TOM LULEVITCH

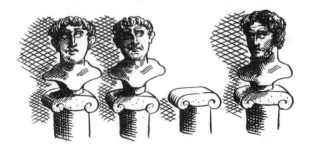

Cader Books

HarperPerennial
A Division of HarperCollins*Publishers*

A hardcover edition of this book was published in 1991 by HarperCollins Publishers, Inc.

Created by Cader Books, 151 East 29th Street, New York, NY 10016.

FIRST HARPERPERENNIAL EDITION published 1994.

Designers: Michael Cader and Michael Macrone

The Library of Congress has catalogued the hardcover edition as follows:

Macrone, Michael.
    It's Greek to me! : brush up your classics / Michael Macrone. — 1st ed.
      p. cm.
    "Cader Books."
    Includes index.
    ISBN 0-06-270022-7
    1. English language—Foreign elements—Greek—Dictionaries. 2. English language—Foreign elements—Latin—Dictionaries. 3. Greek language—Influence on English—Dictionaries. 4. Latin language—Influence on English—Dictionaries. 5. English language—Etymology—Dictionaries.
6. Classical dictionaries. I. Title.
PE1582.G6M3   1991
422'.481—dc20   91-55004

0-06-272044-9 (pbk)
  95 96 97 98 DT/HC 10 9 8 7 6 5 4

Contents

List of Illustrations

Acknowledgments

Covering so broad a stretch of time and so intimidating a list of authors has been cause for humility and trepidation. Had others not paved my way so thoroughly, I should have stumbled almost at the outset.

If I have not conquered the material, I have at least come and seen it, but only with the aid of these reference works: *The Oxford English Dictionary*, 2nd edition (Oxford, 1989); *The Oxford Dictionary of English Proverbs*, 2nd edition (Oxford, 1948); *The Oxford Dictionary of Quotations*, 3rd edition (Oxford, 1979); *The Oxford Classical Dictionary* (Oxford, 1949); *The Oxford Companion to Classical Literature* (Oxford, 1937); *A Classical Dictionary*, by J. Lempriere (London, 1919) (according to Lempriere, the world was created in 4004 B.C.); *Dictionnaire de la Mythologie Grecque et Romaine*, by Pierre Grimal, 2nd edition (Paris, 1958); *A Home Book of Proverbs, Maxims, and Familiar Phrases*, by Burton Stevenson (New York, 1948); *Dictionary of Quotations (Classical)*, by Thomas Benfield Harbottle (London, 1897); *Roman Antiquities*, by Alexander Adam, 12th edition (London, 1835); *Brewer's Dictionary of Phrase and Fable*, revised by Ivor H. Evans (New York, 1959); *Webster's Word Histories* (Springfield, Mass., 1989); *Thereby Hangs a Tale*, by Charles Earle Funk (New York, 1950); *Fabulous Fallacies* (New York, 1982) and *Marvelous Monikers* (New York, 1987), by Tad Tuleja; *Looking at Philosophy*, by Donald Palmer (Mountain View, Calif., 1988); and *The Hammond Historical Atlas of the World* (Maplewood, N.J., 1976).

For well-edited editions of the original texts I have relied heavily on the Loeb Classical Library, now published in the United States by Harvard University Press. For information on my adaptations and translations, see "About the Translations" on page 227.

I should like to thank HarperCollins, in particular my editor Hugh Van Dusen, for supporting the series of books of which this is the second. Stephanie Gunning at HarperCollins has also been of great help in seeing *It's Greek to Me!* through to completion. Finally, I should like above all to acknowledge Michael Cader of Cader Books for his creative and editorial guidance.

MICHAEL MACRONE

Introduction

If you've ever had to admit "It's Greek to me" when asked about the story line of *The Iliad*, *Oedipus the King*, or *The Aeneid* (which might as well be written in Greek), then this book is for you. As you brush up your classics, you will not only reacquaint yourself with the enduring literature, history, and philosophy of ancient civilization, but also discover why the Trojan horse was actually Greek, whether Oedipus had an Oedipus complex, and just how rich Croesus really was.

While you might think Greek and Latin are dead languages, classical ideas and expressions live on—not just in dissertations, high-school mottoes and legal briefs, but even in our everyday speech. IT'S GREEK TO ME! "leaves no stone unturned" (Euripides) in tracing the ancient sources of some of our most colorful colloquial phrases. You'll meet eponymous characters from Mausolus and Mentor to Hector (who was actually a nice guy); cover "the lion's share" (Aesop) of Greek and Roman history; and follow the threads of ancient philosophy, from the essence of Aristotle's "quintessence" to Socrates' "swan song."

If Archimedes were alive today, he'd cry "eureka!" once more to discover that the thumbs-up sign spelled a gladiator's death, that Achilles' Achilles' heel wasn't originally his heel at all, and that long before Alexander Pope wrote "to err is human, to forgive divine," Lucian had set down the same idea in his *Demonax*. In pursuing intriguing etymologies and elucidating stories from ancient times, IT'S GREEK TO ME! cites each phrase in its classical context, revisiting the great works of Homer and Virgil, Ovid and Terence, Plutarch and Aristophanes. More than just a book of word origins, this is a complete tour through the literature, life, and lively expressions of ancient days. And the ride should be more entertaining than the one you got from your Latin teacher.

From Rome to Your Home

Strange as it may seem in our culturally illiterate age, once upon a time the great classical works were more than vaguely familiar to those men and women who sat down to write books. Until about the late eighteenth century, in fact, it was generally agreed that the educated person ought to be equipped with a basic knowledge of ancient languages, and be liberally read in key works by Aristotle, Cicero, Virgil, and Plutarch, among others. So while one can rarely be certain that the coiner of an English version of a classical phrase was quoting the original, chances are that it was lodged somewhere in his memory. Alexander Pope may not have consciously stolen Lucian's words, but it would be mighty surprising if he had never seen them.

Thus tracing the passage of Latin and Greek phrases into English parlance, while not exactly scientific, has neither been an entirely haphazard process. There are cases, though, in which specifying classical sources has presented difficulties. As with most proverbs and catch-phrases, those in Latin and Greek may well have been familiar before they were set down in writing; the oldest surviving record, furthermore, may quote from or paraphrase texts that have been lost. And at times I have been forced to rely on second-hand sources in identifying the coiner or popularizer of a particular phrase.

Nonetheless, I have traced the phrases included here with reasonable probability to specific persons, events, and texts— and if not to the first text, then to the one that most directly inspired the English usage. If you wish, you may take the results, as Pliny the Elder said, "with a grain of salt."

How This Book Is Organized

IT'S GREEK TO ME! begins with Homer because his epics were the first works of Western literature to be written down. The period covered ends at the second century A.D., both because Roman culture was clearly in decline by the third century, and because it is where the interesting material starts running out. (And, by the way, I use the old notation "B.C." and "A.D."— "before Christ" and "*anno domini*" ["year of the Lord"]—rather than "BCE" and "CE"—"before the common era" and "common era," respectively—because it is so well established. I'll never think metrically, either.)

Entries are arranged by their author—Homer, Aesop, etc.— or by subject category, such as "Greek Philosophy" and "Roman History." These sections are arranged in rough chronological order, though there is some overlap—"Greek Philosophy," for example, covers philosophers who lived both before and after Plato. The "Miscellaneous" section includes phrases whose authors neither fell into nor merited full sections.

Phrases Homer coined are arranged by their first appearance in his work; otherwise, an author's phrases are arranged alphabetically. The entries in "Greek History" and "Roman History"— which derive from historical events or figures—are arranged chronologically. The "Greek Drama" and "Roman Drama" sections are broken down chronologically by author, but each author's phrases are for the most part arranged alphabetically. If these arrangements are Greek to you, rest assured that the index is strictly alphabetical.

(You may notice that the book touches very lightly on classical mythology. This is because mythical stories and characters are not the invention of any one author, nor do they concern historical figures and events. Furthermore, I'm saving this ample body of material for my next book.)

Occasionally, one author's work will show up in another section—Plato, for example, contributes to the "Greek Philosophy" section. In such instances I have drawn on these authors in order to clarify or illustrate someone else's coinage when the original was unavailable. There's some flexibility to my categories, but that's in keeping with the spirit of the book.

"There's No Place Like Rome," which follows the main entries, is the home of phrases that lead to Rome (or Greece) but don't clearly begin there, or that required a less detailed exploration than the main entries. (The very expression "All roads lead to Rome" appears to have been coined, not in classical times, but in the seventeenth century). Finally, I have compiled a glossary that supplies biographies and added detail to help you sort out the people, characters, and places of the ancient world. The endpapers of the book contain maps of ancient Greece and Rome that you should also find helpful.

It's Greek to Me!

Homer

(ca. eighth century B.C.)

As the weary Odysseus, delayed once more in his journey home, attends a feast at the court of the Phaecians, a herald ushers in a beautiful singer "beloved above all others by the Muse." Strumming his lyre, the inspired bard chants tales of the heroic deeds of Odysseus at Troy, driving the disguised hero to tears. But the singer does not notice: in return for poetic power, the Muse has exacted his eyesight.

It is tempting to view the blind singer, who appears in Book 8 of Homer's *Odyssey*, as a self-portrait—Homer's representative in an epic tale set five centuries earlier. Homer too, according to legend, was blind; and the Greeks did not doubt that his poetry was inspired by Calliope, the muse of heroic epic. But there is no real evidence that Homer was blind, or even that he existed; and, granting his existence, we cannot be certain that he is responsible for the two great epic poems ascribed to him: the *Iliad* and the *Odyssey*.

If there was a blind bard named Homer, he probably lived in the eighth century B.C. and probably drew on older poems and legends in compiling his lengthy oral epics (Greek writing was developing at about the same time). Probably at some later date, after they were embellished and reshaped by other singers, the *Iliad* and *Odyssey* were written down and attributed solely to Homer.

These two works are the first recorded epic poems—that is, long verse narratives concerning the wonderful deeds of great heroes and gods, recited in a high style. The *Iliad* describes a brief period in the ten-year war between Greece and Troy, a kingdom on the northeast coast of Asia Minor (now Turkey) whose capital Ilium is fated to go down in flames. The poem's central subject is the wrath of Achilles, the great Greek warrior who deserts the battlefield after a spat with his commander Agamemnon. The *Odyssey*, whose style and subject are very different, picks up the story of Odysseus, king of the Greek island of Ithaca, some ten years after the fall of Troy. Where the *Iliad* recounts the public deeds of great combatants guided by their contentious gods, the *Odyssey* describes the private tribulations of a man seeking a way home, where his wife Penelope weaves a shroud for her father-in-law and attempts to fend off numerous would-be husbands.

The Trojan War

"O would to God the day
That first gave light to me had been a whirlwind,
And borne me to some desert hill, or hid me in the rage
Of earth's farthest seas, rather than I should so endanger
The dear lives of so many friends. Since the Gods have been
Sole foreseers of my plagues, they might likewise have seen
That, to bear out their award, they had yoked me
To a man of more spirit. . . .
    "But come, good brother Hector, rest you here,
You who, of the world of men, suffers most for me,
Vile wretch, and for my lover's wrong—on whom a destiny
So bitter is imposed by Zeus that all succeeding times
Will put, to our unending shames, our crimes in all men's mouths."

Homer, *Iliad*, Book 6, lines 345–358

This is the complaint of the woman we call Helen of Troy, who is actually a Greek, daughter of Zeus and the mortal Leda. As you probably know, she was the cause of the Trojan War, but the reasons are complex and less familiar. Pieced together from various accounts, the story goes something like this:

When the Trojan prince Paris was still in the womb, his mother Hecuba dreamt that her child would be the torch that set fire to Troy, their kingdom in northwest Asia Minor. King Priam, alarmed at this and at similar warnings from the local soothsayers, ordered the child destroyed immediately upon its birth. As often happens in stories like this, the child did not die, but was rescued by shepherds and raised as their own.

Meanwhile, the goddesses quarreled over a certain golden apple inscribed with the motto "Property of the Most Beautiful." All claimants but three were eliminated, leaving Hera (queen of the gods), Aphrodite (goddess of love), and Athena (goddess of wisdom). When the squabble finally got on Zeus's nerves, he ordered the three to take their case to Paris, who assumed the unenviable burden of deciding which goddess deserved the apple. Each proffered a bribe; Paris eventually decided to take up Aphrodite's offer of the most beautiful woman in the world. She got the apple, and he got Helen. But there was a catch: Helen was already married to Menelaus, king of Sparta.

Paris eventually made his way, with his new wife, back to Troy, where he was reconciled with his parents. What might have been only a showdown between two men over one woman then escalated into full-scale war between the united Greek kingdoms and Troy. And though he was the cause of all this grief, Paris turned out to be, at least according to Homer, pretty useless as a warrior. Thus Helen's complaint that if the gods insisted on making her the cause of a war, they could at least have provided her a lover with some spirit.

Hecuba's dream eventually came true, when, with the help of their Trojan Horse [*see* p. 13], the Greeks burned Troy to a crisp. And as Helen predicts, the story of her and Paris's "crimes" do become the talk of "all succeeding times," especially Homer's. It's doubtful that, if Helen and Paris existed, their crimes were exactly as Homer describes them; but there may be some historical basis for tales of the war. Excavations have uncovered a stratum of ruins—called "Troy VIIA"—left by a fire at about the time of the legendary Trojan War, circa 1250 B.C.

To Bite the Dust

"O Zeus, most great, most glorious, that sits amidst the stars
And the dark clouds, do not let the sun go down
And surrender to darkness till I have with my own hands
Overthrown and burned the palace of Priam,
And with my sword pierced Hector's breast,
And until thousands who share with him in this quarrel
Fall headlong in the dust and bite the earth."

Homer, Iliad, Book 2, lines 412–418

The Greeks, having recently suffered setbacks in the war with Troy, have retreated to their camp to fret over their champion Achilles' retirement from battle. But Zeus determines to shake the Greeks out of their defeatism, and so he sends a dream to their commander Agamemnon that promises them almost instant victory over Troy if they act quickly.

Though Zeus is promising more than he intends to deliver, the dream does produce the desired effect: the Greeks assemble a war council at which they determine to march back out for more punishment. Agamemnon gives the speech quoted here, in which he foresees thousands of Trojans "falling in the dust and biting the earth." This phrase is one of Homer's favorites, and seems to have been a popular Greek metaphor for inglorious death in battle.

The English phrase "to bite the dust" originated in an 1870 translation of this passage, though "bite the ground" appears earlier. The latter may derive from Homer or perhaps from Virgil, who uses it in a part of his *Aeneid* modeled on the *Iliad*.

Pygmies

When the soldiers had obeyed every last command,
And both sides were set to fight, the Trojans came upon
The Greeks with rude noises, crying out like the cranes
That fill the air with harsh confusion, and, escaping winter's storms,
Brutishly clamor as they soar upon the ocean in ridiculous war,
Visiting death upon the Pygmaian men.

Homer, *Iliad*, Book 3, lines 1–7

Homer alludes here to a legend that so-called Pygmies inhabited southern Egypt or Ethiopia, where they fortified themselves against hostile storks or cranes. Homer likens the clamoring Trojans, as they visit war and confusion upon the Pygmy-like Greeks, to these cranes. ("Pygmy" derives from the Greek *pygmaios*, "dwarfish," itself deriving from *pygme*, "the distance from one's elbow to his knuckles.")

Some legends trace the crane/Pygmy conflict to the impiety of Oenoe, a beautiful maid who married a Pygmy, only to be turned into a stork by Hera, jealous queen of the gods. Oenoe flies about searching for her son, and when she grabs him in her beak the Pygmies, not knowing who she is, attack her. The other storks launch a counter-attack, and thus begins the war.

"Pygmy" was already an English synonym for "dwarfish" when in the late nineteenth century small nomadic peoples were discovered inhabiting equatorial Africa. These tribes were thought to be the same *pygmaios* referred to by Homer and later by Herodotus and Virgil. Thus the name "pygmy" was transferred to them, though Europeans had come to believe that the ancient legends referred to dwarfish inhabitants of eastern India.

Stentorian

Amidst all the admiring throng,
Hera took on the shape of Stentor, he of the brazen voice
Who spoke as loud as fifty men. She shouted out like him
And chided the Argives: "O ye Greeks—princes only in name
And outward rite, not in act—what scandal do you do to honor?"

Homer, *Iliad*, Book 5, lines 784–787

At this point the Trojan War has turned in the Trojans' favor, with the help of the war-god Ares. As the Greeks ("Argives") lick their wounds, their chief divine advocate arrives on the scene: Hera, queen of the gods. In order to rouse them from their stupor, Hera takes on the shape and speech of the Greek herald Stentor, a man whose voice is like bronze and as loud as fifty normal voices. Stentor may be forgotten in the rest of the *Iliad*, but the Greeks remembered Homer's lines, and "to shout louder than Stentor" became a common proverb.

As George Chapman began gradually publishing in the late sixteenth century the first English translation of Homer, his contemporaries started finding uses for the name "Stentor." Thomas Nashe refers to him in 1600; playwright Ben Jonson has his noise-hating misanthrope Morose, in *Epicoene* (1609), cry upon the revelers who have invaded his house as "Rogues, hell-hounds, Stentors, . . . sons of noise and tumult" (Act 4, scene 2).

From "Stentor" we have derived the adjective "stentorian," which originally meant "loud, booming," as applied to someone's voice. "Stentorian" later came to refer to instruments and to people with stentorian voices.

Eat Your Heart Out

"The princess bore Bellerophon three children,
Isandros and Hippolochos and fair Laodameia,
With whom even Zeus left heaven to lie
And to beget by her the helmeted Sarpedon, called divine.
But, lest a mere man should share their glory,
The gods turned against Bellerophon,
And he wandered evermore through this Aleian field,
Eating his heart out, fleeing the loathed company of men."

Homer, *Iliad*, Book 6, lines 196–202

Homer's expression "eating his heart out"—he will use the phrase repeatedly in the *Odyssey*—here describes the gnawing despair of the legendary hero Bellerophon. It seems to have entered English by way of the Latin version, *cor ne edito* ("do not eat your heart"), which the great humanist Erasmus of Rotterdam transmitted to the Renaissance. In 1539 Richard Taverner translated Erasmus this way: "Eat not thy heart; that is to say, consume not thy self with cares." The phrase quickly became popular; but somehow it's been transformed from a piece of advice into an annoying crow of triumph. "Eat your heart out!" cries the victor to the vanquished, flaunting his spoils. You may wish to punch this individual in the face, but don't blame Homer for inventing the brag.

Bellerophon had good reason to "eat his heart out," which is why he made such interesting material for writers like Homer, Hesiod, Sophocles, and Euripides, who could always use a good story of senseless misfortune. As the story goes, Bellerophon, endowed by the gods with beauty and "desirable manhood," found his manhood drawing unwanted attention from Anteia, wife of King Proteus of Argos. Bellerophon resists, so in revenge Anteia accuses him of attempted rape. Proteus sends Bellerophon to Anteia's father, King Iobates of Lykia, instructing our hero to convey a tablet to the king. Inscribed on this tablet are secret instructions to have Bellerophon killed.

That's just the beginning. Iobates sends Bellerophon off to what he assumes will be certain death, charging him to kill the monstrous Chimera. Not only does Bellerophon succeed, he survives several other deadly traps, so Iobates is forced to give up, and he offers Bellerophon his daughter's hand. This is where we come in: Bellerophon fathers three children, whose own children will go on to star in the Trojan War.

But after the gods see Bellerophon through all these trials, they suddenly turn on him in a fit of jealousy. Ares and Artemis arrange for the deaths of his children Isandros and Laodameia, respectively, and Bellerophon is left wandering the plain of Aleios (in Asia), "eating his heart out."

To Hector

"Patroclus, your conceit gave you the overthrow of Troy,
And your fleet a freight of Trojan women, stripped of their freedom;
But you prized yourself too highly, and I have blocked all your plans.
To halt them my horses have stretched forth their hooves into this war,
And I, best by far among Trojans at arms, hold off from Troy—
Even to the last beam of my life—their day of necessity."

Homer, Iliad, Book 16, lines 830–836

Hector doesn't really "hector." The word may be derived from the Trojan hero's name, but, while we use it to mean "bully, bluster, intimidate," Hector is generally a polite and honorable fellow. On the other hand, he does brag now and again, especially after he's planted his spear in the belly of Patroclus, one of Greece's top warriors. Patroclus, incredibly, is not impressed, and he sneers at Hector's "big words"—it was fate, after all, and not Hector, that decreed he should die. Patroclus furthermore warns the Trojan that his own death is close by, which turns out to be true, since Achilles will soon avenge his dear friend's death.

The modern sense of "hector" seems to derive from a group of seventeenth-century London street-toughs known as "Hectors." These sword-wielding window-breakers probably gave themselves this name, flattering their own prowess; but everyone else in the city regarded them as blustering bullies.

An Odyssey

Reveal, O Muse, that man of wisdom, and of many ways,
That wandered wondrous far after he had sacked
And brought to ruin the sacred city of Troy.
He saw the cities of a world of nations,
With all their manners, minds, and fashions;
At sea he suffered many woes, and spent much care
To save himself and his men from overthrows
As they made their way home.

Homer, *Odyssey*, Book 1, lines 1–5

In the opening lines of his *Odyssey,* Homer advertises the strange, wonderful, and very lengthy adventures Odysseus will face on his trip home from the Trojan War. The far-flung itinerary, the variety of experiences, the triumphs and tribulations, the amateur anthropology: all these are at the roots of our idea of an "odyssey."

Homer's book is, of course, named after its hero Odysseus, or Ulysses—just as the *Iliad* is named after Ilios, or Troy. Both titles, and the *Odyssey* in particular, have become common nouns in English, though "iliad" is very rare and Homer is never forgotten when it's spoken. Surprisingly, "odyssey"—which now means "journey of discovery" or "spiritual quest"—didn't appear as a common noun until the late nineteenth century, when it meant simply "wayward travel." Odysseus's odyssey is certainly that; yet there's some justice in our more spiritualized use of the term, since Odysseus, as he makes his toilsome way back to his home in Ithaca, discovers many things about himself as well as about the natural and supernatural worlds.

A Mentor

After Telemachus had spoken, Mentor arose,
The close companion to whom Odysseus,
When he set forth, had entrusted his family,
And charged to keep all safe till his return.

Homer, Odyssey, Book 2, lines 224–227

Mentor was a good and trusty friend, but he didn't really turn into a *mensch* until the eighteenth century. In Homer's *Odyssey*, he is one of the few inhabitants of Ithaca who remain loyal to King Odysseus, now widely presumed dead—after all, it's been ten years since the end of the Trojan War and the king hasn't been heard from since. For now, Mentor fights a losing battle against the common opinion, according to which Odysseus's wife Penelope ought to accept her husband's death and marry one of the pushy suitors who have turned her house into a daily riot.

Mentor himself plays no role in the rest of the tale, but the goddess Athena takes on the old man's guise so as to liberally bestow her superior advice on Odysseus's son Telemachus and on Odysseus himself, helping them arrange the ultimate defeat of the suitors.

In 1699, Archbishop Fénelon of Cambrai adapted the story of Telemachus in his novel *Télémaque*, ditching Athena and building up the character of Mentor himself. This admirable figure soon became synonymous with wise counsel, first in France and then in England. Lord Chesterfield wrote to his son in 1730 of the "friendly care and assistance of your Mentor"—straddling the line between invoking the character and employing a common noun. By the 1870s, "mentor" was written with a lower-case *m* and had thus finally detached itself from Homer's story.

A Trojan Horse

The Greeks boarded their ships,
Having set all their tents on fire; yet other kings,
In great Odysseus's command, hid in the horse
In Troy's vast marketplace, whence the Trojans
Drew it up to Ilium; there, they sat about it,
And debated on how to dispose the gift.

Homer, *Odyssey*, Book 8, lines 500–506

The famous story of the Trojan horse—which is actually a Greek horse, built with the help of the goddess Athena—exists in many versions, but Homer's is the first one written down. As he tells the story, the Greeks make a show of abandoning their camp and thus giving up the war with Troy [*see* p. 3], but they have a trick up their sleeves. At the urging of Odysseus, they build a hollow horse, fill it with their top warriors, and leave it in the assembly-place or marketplace of Troy.

The Trojans drag this "gift" into their city, but are unsure what to do with it. Some counsel hacking open the horse; others propose pushing it off a cliff; still others think it should be left in place as a dedication to the gods for their help in defeating the Greeks. The last course prevails, but the gods have other plans; in fact, they have fated that Troy should burn. When all is safe, the Greeks jump out of the horse and, without pity, destroy the town.

Homer's account is less judgmental than later ones, such as Virgil's, which look dimly on the Greeks' subterfuge. Virgil makes much of some Trojans' suspicions, having Laocoön, a priest of Neptune, incredulously demand whether "any gift of Greece" could be "free of guile"—"Is this what Ulysses is known for?" (Romans and Europeans called Odysseus "Ulysses.") "I fear the Greeks," he concludes, "even when they bear gifts" (*Aeneid*, Book 2). Laocoön's warning goes unheeded, but his words have been immortalized in the English proverb "Beware of Greeks bearing gifts."

Most everywhere in Europe, whose people once fancied themselves descendants of the Trojans, Ulysses and his "Trojan horse" were long regarded as evil. Dante and his guide Virgil find Ulysses consigned to the eighth circle of hell, and Virgil moralizes on the Greek's evil counsel, his "craft" in devising "the ambush of the horse" (*Inferno*, canto 26). In medieval times, Ulysses was also condemned for his supposed curiosity, his legendary travels having come to represent impious searching beyond what man was meant to know. But as the Renaissance rediscovered individualism and science, Ulysses was gradually rehabilitated, though his role in devising the Trojan horse has yet to be fully forgiven. We are still admonished to beware of Greeks bearing gifts.

A Windbag

"In the hide of a nine-year-old ox, Aeolus enfolded
The airy blasts of all the stormy winds;
For Zeus had made him steward of the winds,
Giving him power to raise and calm them.
And these he gave me, thus curbed of their rage."

Homer, *Odyssey*, Book 10, lines 19–22

Some readers may think of Homer himself as a windbag, but if so it's not his fault, as this story will prove. As he rests at the court of Alcinous, king of the Phaecians [*see* p. 1], Odysseus describes stopping by the floating island of Aeolus, a man loved by the gods and entrusted by Zeus with the keeping of the winds. When Odysseus asks for help in speeding his way home, Aeolus obliges by giving him a windbag—an oxhide stuffed with "airy blasts." The bag is supposed to act as a kind of charm, preventing storms and maintaining a good west wind. But Odysseus's greedy crew, thinking the bag full of gold, untie it and thus unleash a storm that blows the ship back to the island. Aeolus throws Odysseus and his men out, certain that they're hated by the gods.

Thus the first windbag in literature. However, though "windbag" did come to refer in English to such a charm, the word was first used (in the fifteenth century) to name the bellows of an organ. Later one's "windbags" were his or her lungs, and finally a "windbag" was a pretentious braggart. The proverb "words are but wind" appears as early as the thirteenth century, but it wasn't until the nineteenth that someone full of hot air was called a windbag.

The Argonauts

"Never could a ship shun the perils of that pass,
But ran upon the rocks, to the utter ruin of ship and men;
For the seas there are furious, and whirlwinds of fire rage.
Only the *Argo*—a ship in all men's thoughts—passed through,
On its return from Aeta. Yet even she had been wrecked
Had Hera not lent her hand, out of love for Jason."

Homer, *Odyssey*, Book 12, lines 66–72

With this depressing news, Circe makes Odysseus's trip home, including a courtesy call on Teiresias in hell, sound as untenable as possible [*see* A SIREN SONG]. She is describing the passage between Sicily and the Italian mainland, which is so rocky and treacherous that only one ship has ever made it through: the *Argo*, with Jason at the helm, the Argonauts on deck, and the goddess Hera up above. Homer provides no more of Jason's history, but he became an extremely popular figure in later literature as various authors told and retold the tale of his quest for the Golden Fleece.

According to the definitive account, in Pindar's *Fourth Pythian Ode* (ca. 462 B.C.), the golden fleece of a ram has been preserved

at Colchis, at the east end of the Black Sea, and set under the watch of a fierce dragon. Jason must recover this fleece in order to regain the throne of Iolcos, in Thessaly, which is now in the hands of his uncle Pelias. So Jason sets out with his Argonauts, and many a thrilling adventure ensues. He eventually recovers the fleece with the help of Medea, princess of Colchis, who loves but is later abandoned by him, much to her fury. In one version of the tale, Jason meets his end when, as he reposes under the *Argo*, a piece of the ship falls and kills him.

It is sometimes supposed that the English word "argosy" refers to Jason's famous adventures. Actually, "argosy" derives from the Italian *Ragusea*, that is, a vessel hailing from Ragusa— not the Sicilian town, but the Yugoslavian port now known as Dubrovnik. First written in Renaissance English as "Arragosa," "argosy" came to mean "a very large merchant vessel," and later "a fleet of ships." (Jason's *Argo* itself was named after its builder, Argos, whose name signifies "rapid" in Greek.) Jason's story is, however, the source of the nickname "Argonaut," bestowed on those seekers who ventured to California in 1849, at the height of the great Gold Rush.

A Siren Song

"First you shall meet with the Sirens, who capture the minds
Of all whom they can acquaint with their attractions.
Whoever shall approach them unforewarned
And heed their song will never again turn
His affection home, and will despise
His wife and children, as they gather to greet him—
The Sirens will so enchant him with their song,
Shrill, and yet powerfully sensual."

Homer, *Odyssey*, Book 12, lines 39–44

Odysseus is having a devil of a time getting home to his wife and son. He is finally slipping out of Circe's clutches, and now she tells him to expect more trouble, though he's already had plenty. Lying in wait ahead on the high seas is a group of Sirens, extremely attractive creatures whose alluring songs make passersby forget all about the wife and kids. Circe advises Odysseus to have his men stop their ears with wax; but if he wants to enjoy the Sirens' little concert, he should have himself bound tight to a mast so he won't jump overboard and swim their way. This plan does succeed, contrary to subsequent versions of the legend in which Odysseus succumbs.

Numerous later writers were fascinated with the Sirens, who perhaps seemed a perfect metaphor for their inexplicable attraction to women. Plato, not a man with much affection for the opposite sex [*see* PLATONIC LOVE], tells in the *Republic* of the hero Er, who returns from death to relate his vision of the netherworld. Among the figures he encounters are eight Sirens, whose song is ethereal rather than enticing. Yet in the *Cratylus* they reappear as seducers who are themselves the victims of desire. Love conquers all [*see* p. 140].

The word "*sirenes*" later popped up in the Latin version of Isaiah, chapter 13, rendering a Hebrew word that means something like "jackals." Because the earliest English translators thought Isaiah meant flying serpents, "siren" was first used to name these horrible beasts. Chaucer, on the other hand, thought that when the French talked about *sirènes*, they meant mermaids, where in Homer they're half woman and half bird, not half fish.

"Siren song" itself appears in English by the sixteenth century, when Roger Ascham, the tutor of Queen Elizabeth, compared Catholic Italy to a treacherous sea; he praised those "Noble personages . . . whom all the Siren songs of Italy could never untwine from the mast of God's word." "Siren song" was thereafter synonymous with a deceitful lure, enchanting to the ear yet deadly in its effects.

But not all "siren songs" sound so pleasant. In 1819 the Frenchman Charles de la Tour invented a device for producing a piercing tone by rotating a perforated disk in a stream of water. Homer's sea-dwelling monsters came immediately to mind, and he dubbed his invention a "siren." Later, the name was given to the factory whistle that summoned laborers to work—a deadly song, indeed, but hardly sweet. From there, "siren" was applied to a variety of maddening noises meant to jar people out of their pleasant mood rather than to lure them into complacence. As a word for songs that put us on guard rather than off, "siren" has come to mean just the opposite of what Homer meant.

Scylla and Charybdis

"Here the wailing Scylla shrouds her face, whose cries
Are no louder than a new-born kitten's, though
She herself is a monster. . . .
She has twelve foul feet; six huge necks extend
From her rank shoulders; and upon each neck
A ghastly head; every head is thickly set
With three rows of abhorred teeth; every tooth
Is stuck with black death. . . .
You shall then see the humbler rock, so close by
That you could measure the distance with a dart.
Upon it is a huge fig tree, ample with leaves,
Beneath whose shade divine Charybdis sits,
Drinking up the black deep. Three times a day
She drinks the pit dry, and three times a day
She belches it up again."

Homer, *Odyssey*, Book 12, lines 85–87, 89–92, 101–106

The Sirens were bad enough [*see* p. 18]. After Odysseus is through with them, Circe says, he must make his way through the Straits of Messina by sailing past Scylla and Charybdis, and it's hard to say which is worse. Scylla, who lives in a cave on a high rock, is a six-headed monster who thinks every time is lunchtime. Every one of her six mouths is equipped with three rows of teeth, and whenever a ship happens by she pokes her heads out of the cave and snaps up a catch with each ghastly maw.

Nearby, under a lower cliff, Charybdis, a sort of deified whirlpool, is at work, sucking down water three times a day, and with it anything else in the neighborhood. Circe recommends going for Scylla; that way, Odysseus only loses six men instead of his whole ship. Odysseus agrees, and decides he won't tell his crew about what's in store, lest they decide that life with the Sirens sounds pretty good.

Though Homer makes it clear that Charybdis, while less unpleasant looking, is worse, modern writers treat the two as

equally dire alternatives—the classical rock and a hard place. The Romantic poet Shelley, for example, wrote in *A Defense of Poetry* (1821) that "The rich have become richer, and the poor have become poorer; and the vessel of the state is driven between the Scylla and Charybdis of anarchy and despotism." The options seem equally bad. Earlier English writers were a little more careful with Homer's text; in 1580 William Spelman specified, correctly, that "I fell from Scylla into Charybdis, from evil into worse."

Sardonic

With that Ktesippos hurled a cow's foot
At Odysseus's head, but he turned away
And dodged the blow. Then Odysseus smiled
A sardonic smile; but Telemachus
Could not disguise his anger.

Homer, *Odyssey*, Book 20, lines 299–303

Odysseus has just about had enough of the arrogant men who, thinking him dead, have rudely occupied his household in an attempt to convince his wife Penelope to take one of them as a husband. One of the worst of the lot is Ktesippos, a man well-schooled in villainy; in order to abuse an elderly visitor, who is actually Odysseus in disguise, Ktesippos offers him a gift—which turns out to be an ox hoof launched at Odysseus's head. All hell is about to break loose, but for now Odysseus restrains his anger beneath a "sardonic smile."

The Greek *sardanios*, which Homer uses here, means "bitter or scornful," but it later merged with *sardonios*, Sardinian—a merger which has put etymologists to some trouble. Later writers thought that "sardonic" referred to the effects of eating a bitter plant, called in Latin *herba Sardonia*, native to the island of Sardinia. Legendarily, ingesting this herb produced severe facial contortions and later death; so "sardonic laughter" was equated with Sardonian symptoms. Appropriately enough, the goddess Athena, finally intervening on behalf of the sardonic Odysseus, forces the wicked suitors to laugh uncontrollably and painfully, then spurs them on to violent acts that do indeed bring death upon them.

AESOP

(sixth century B.C.)

You know about the race between the tortoise and the hare, and about the boy who cried "wolf!" But Aesop, the man who invented them, is as obscure as his fables are famous. Here is what we know: The Greek historian Herodotus claims Aesop was a slave. Plato says that his master Socrates versified a few of Aesop's fables while in prison. Plato's student Aristotle tells us that Aesop once spoke in defense of a popular leader on the island of Samos; if so, the fable-writer was by then no longer a slave. Plutarch adds that Aesop was so esteemed by the Lydian king Croesus [*see* p. 43] that the latter sent him on a deputation to the oracle at Delphi [*see* ORACULAR].

Such indirect testimony is all we have to go by, so it is difficult to prove or disprove the many legends about Aesop—that he was quite ugly, for instance, or that he was born in Phrygia, or that he met his end when the Delphians threw him over a precipice. Aesop's life—perhaps even Aesop himself—may be a kind of fable. The texts I use here may indeed have been in Aesop's repertoire, but if so they may not have been original to him and have certainly been rewritten and embellished in later times. (Some of "Aesop's" fables, for example, have been found in Egyptian texts from the previous millennium.)

Most Greek fables, like those of other ancient cultures, are animal stories with a human, and sometimes obscurely political, moral. Some, however, have human characters, and some lack animals altogether—"The Milkmaid and Her Pail," for example [*see* p. 25]. But whatever the subject matter, all the fables use concrete incidents to briefly convey wry observations on human behavior.

To Blow Hot and Cold

A man and a satyr became friends, and determined to live together. All went well for a while, until one day in winter-time the satyr saw the man blowing on his hands. "Why do you do that?" he asked. "To warm my hands," said the man. That same day, when they sat down to supper together, they each had a steaming hot bowl of porridge, and the man raised his bowl to his mouth and blew on it. "Why do you do that?" asked the satyr. "To cool my porridge," said the man. The satyr got up from the table. "Good-bye," said he, "I'm going: I can't be friends with a man who blows hot and cold with the same breath."

Aesop, "The Man and the Satyr"

Satyrs are mythological fertility figures, half man and half goat, who are supposed to have served the wine-god Bacchus. And as the attendant of a god, Aesop's satyr is rather ignorant of curious human customs. (Substitute "Martian" for "satyr" for a quick update.) That his human friend can "blow hot and cold with the same breath" strikes the monster as monstrous, and thus ends their fragile friendship.

As usual, Aesop's concrete tale points to a more abstract conclusion. In this case, it seems that the confused satyr is the butt of a joke—he can't reconcile himself to local customs that may seem contradictory, but aren't. Through the years Aesop's image has taken on a much more literal meaning. Now we use blowing hot and cold as a metaphor for true inconsistency; it means to vacillate, or to bluster one moment and humble one-self the next. The metaphor appeared in written English by the sixteenth century, when one writer, for example, said that "These men can blow hot and cold out of the same mouth to serve several purposes."

Don't Count Your Chickens

A farmer's daughter had been out to milk the cows, and was returning to the dairy carrying her pail of milk upon her head. As she walked along, she fell a-musing after this fashion: "The milk in this pail will provide me with cream, which I will make into butter and take to market to sell. With the money I will buy a number of eggs, and these, when hatched, will produce chickens, and by and by I shall have quite a large poultry-yard."

Aesop, "The Milkmaid and Her Pail"

You probably remember what happens to Aesop's milkmaid. Each calculation she makes, based on the previous one, is more fantastic. The milk will yield her cream, the cream butter, the butter eggs, the eggs chickens; the chickens will earn her money for a gown, the gown will win her the attention of all the young fellows of the village, and their suits will only earn them her scorn—"I shall toss my head and have nothing to say to them." Her delusions of grandeur so overcome her that she forgets about the pail of milk, the one thing she actually possesses. When she tosses her head at her imagined suitors, the milk is spilled, and thus ends her brilliant career.

By "counting her chickens before they're hatched"—to paraphrase Aesop's tale—the milkmaid stakes her future on events which are, at best, chancy. We use the phrase to warn someone that she shouldn't start reaping tomorrow's benefits before today's work is successfully completed. Aesop's fairly obvious moral, which almost every schoolchild finds familiar, has been disregarded time and time again. Substitute your favorite corporate raider for the milkmaid and suddenly Aesop seems the stuff of contemporary headlines.

Fascist

A father whose sons were perpetually quarreling decided to give them a practical illustration of the evils of disunion. He gave to each in succession a bundle of sticks and ordered them to break it. Though each son tried with all his strength, none succeeded. The father then unbound the sticks and gave each son one of them, which they broke easily. Then he said: "My sons, if you are of one mind, and unite to assist each other, you will be as this bundle, proof against your enemies. But if you are divided among yourselves, you will be broken as easily as these sticks."

Aesop, "The Bundle of Sticks"

When the patriot John Dickinson famously wrote, in his "Liberty Song" of 1768, that "By uniting we stand, by dividing we fall," he was applying to the American colonists' cause an idea first illustrated by Aesop, and later appropriated by everyone from Etruscan kings to Benito Mussolini. Attendants of Roman officials carried bundles of elm or birch rods tied around an axe as a symbol of authority, as well as a symbol of the people's strength in unity. This bundle, called a *fascis* (plural *fasces*), was thus an emblem of state power. So it is today—twin *fasces* are mounted to either side of the Speaker's chair in the U.S. House of Representatives. A *fascis* also once adorned the reverse of the U.S. dime.

From the Latin word *fascis* came the Italian *fasci*, "bundles, groups," which in the late nineteenth century came to mean "political groupings." Aesop's idea of "strength in unity" was joined to the *fascis* icon by Mussolini, who organized in 1919 a group of political radicals and outcasts in the *Partito Nazionale Fascista*. This group, which followed in the nationalistic, anti-Bolshevist tradition of earlier *fasci*, took power in Italy in 1922. And this is the group that, in 1921, first became known in English as "fascists."

The Goose That Laid the Golden Eggs

A man and his wife had the good fortune to possess a goose which laid a golden egg every day. Lucky though they were, they soon began to think they were not getting rich fast enough, and, imagining the bird must be made of gold inside, they decided to kill it in order to secure the whole store of precious metal at once. But when they cut it open they found it was just like any other goose. Thus they neither got rich all at once, as they had hoped, nor enjoyed any longer the daily addition to their wealth.

Aesop, "The Goose That Laid the Golden Eggs"

This is a classic story of greed, which will likely survive in proverb form as long as that vice does. The foolish couple, not content with riches piecemeal, imagine that what produces wealth must already have the wealth inside it. It is of course the goose's biological functions that produce the gold, and killing it puts a stop to all its biological functions.

In current usage, "to kill the goose that lays the golden eggs" is to foolishly ruin a handsomely profitable enterprise, whether or not the butcher's intention is to make a quicker profit. Many leveraged buyouts, for example, seek to preserve the gold while auctioning off the goose parts, somewhat the reverse of our milkmaid's business strategy [*see* p. 25]. Perhaps the modern lesson is to take the cash cow over the productive chicken or the glittering goose.

Actually, the fable, first rendered into English in 1484, has long offered financial metaphors. As the *Spectator*, for example, remarked in 1911, "Capital already committed to an industry can sometimes be 'held up' by the State and forced to accept, not the market price, but a price artificially fixed. . . . Such treatment soon kills the goose that lays the golden eggs."

The Lion's Share

A lion and a wild ass went out hunting together: the latter was to run down
the prey by his superior speed, and the former would then come up and
dispatch it. They met with great success; and when it came to sharing the
spoil the Lion divided it all into three equal portions. "I will take the first,"
said he, "because I am King of the beasts; I will also take the second,
because, as your partner, I am entitled to half of what remains; and as for
the third—well, unless you give it up to me and get out of here fast, the
third, believe me, will make you feel very sorry for yourself!"

Aesop, "The Lion and the Wild Ass"

In Aesop's fable, the lion's share of the spoils is *all* the spoils.
What the lion doesn't claim by virtue of ruling the beasts, he
claims as his share from the partnership; the remainder he
merely seizes by might. In other words, "might makes right" [*see*
p. 90]—a moral attached to the fable by some translators. We, on
the other hand, mean by "the lion's share" not the whole thing,
but only the greater portion. And we don't necessarily imply that
the lion simply grabs his share; he might earn it, inherit it, or
assume it by default—indeed, it may even be his burden.

The actual English phrase "the lion's share" has been traced
only as far back as Edmund Burke's sobering *Reflections on the
Revolution in France* (1790), but
it appears frequently in nineteenth-century writings. The
magazine *Punch*, for example,
provided instructions in its June
22, 1872 issue on "The art of
finding a rich friend to make a
tour with you in autumn, and of
leaving him to bear the lion's
share of the expenses."

Put Your Shoulder to the Wheel

A wagoner was driving his team along a muddy lane with a full load behind them, when the wheels of his wagon sank so deep in the mire that his horses could by no effort move them. As he stood there, looking helplessly on and calling loudly at intervals upon Hercules for assistance, the god himself appeared and said to him, "Put your shoulder to the wheel, man, and goad on your horses, and then you may call on Hercules to assist you. If you won't lift a finger to help yourself, you can't expect Hercules or any one else to come to your aid."

Aesop, "Hercules and the Wagoner"

Hercules, not the most generous member of the Greek pantheon, refuses here to pull a wagon out of the mud unless the wagoner takes the initiative. Hercules orders the hapless man to "Put your shoulder to the wheel," and thus coins a phrase we've all heard a little too often.

Although Aesop doesn't tell us whether the wagoner complies, the first Englishman to cite the phrase in print was happy to finish the story. Robert Burton, in his delightful *Anatomy of Melancholy* (1621), quotes Hercules in Latin and concludes that the wagoner "whipped his horses withal, and put his shoulder to the wheel." Aesop, a most economical storyteller, was content simply to present the option, holding open the possibility of leaving the wagon in the mire and writing off the loss as a business expense.

The moral, "the gods help those that help themselves," was added to the fable by later translators. The English version probably derives from the Latin saying "the gods help those who do," and was recorded by the mid-sixteenth century. We owe the current form to Benjamin Franklin, who wrote, in his 1736 almanac, "God helps them that help themselves."

Sour Grapes

A hungry fox saw some fine bunches of grapes hanging from a vine that was trained along a high trellis, and did his best to reach them by jumping as high as he could into the air. But it was all in vain, for they were just out of reach. So the fox gave up trying and walked away with an air of dignity and unconcern, remarking, "I thought those grapes were ripe, but I see now they are quite sour."

Aesop, "The Fox and the Grapes"

There's never been a lack of hungry foxes in human society, and they continue to behave much like Aesop's. By "sour grapes" we refer to that telling bitterness in the face of defeat when what someone (always someone else) desires exceeds his grasp.

Aesop's tale of the sour grapes is sometimes confused with a famous line from the Biblical Book of Jeremiah (31:29): "the fathers have eaten a sour grape, and the children's teeth are set on edge." But these fathers have had no trouble satisfying their desires; in fact, their licentious indulgences are the source of the children's misery. The Jews' "teeth are set on edge" by the grapes their fathers have eaten, which tasted good going down but seem bitter to the next generation, who bear the brunt of Jehovah's displeasure.

Shakespeare refers to the fable—first translated in the fifteenth century—in *All's Well that Ends Well,* where a courtier taunts the ailing king of France for refusing treatment he thinks is useless: "O, will you eat/ No grapes, my royal fox? Yes, but you will/ My noble grapes, and if my royal fox/ Could reach them" (Act 2, scene 1).

A Wolf in Sheep's Clothing

A wolf resolved to disguise himself in order that he might prey upon a flock of sheep without fear of detection. So he clothed himself in a sheepskin and slipped among the sheep when they were out at pasture. He completely deceived the shepherd, and when the flock was penned for the night he was shut in with the rest.

Aesop, "The Wolf in Sheep's Clothing"

If you know Aesop, you'll expect an ironic ending to this tale, and you get one. The shepherd, fancying mutton for dinner, enters the pen and lays hands on the wolf, putting him to the blade on the spot. The wolf's comeuppance is quite satisfying, but it is not usually in mind when we call somebody "a wolf in sheep's clothing." Perhaps we're more pessimistic than Aesop.

Although Aesop is the ultimate source of the phrase, it may, like "sour grapes," have gained some prestige from its appearance in the Bible. In his Sermon on the Mount (Matthew 7:15), first put into English in the fourteenth century, Jesus warns his audience to "Beware of false prophets, which come to you in sheep's clothing, but inwardly they are ravening wolves." And, again like "sour grapes," the phrase has profited by a Shakespearean allusion. In *King Henry the Sixth, Part 1*, the Duke of Gloucester cries to the Bishop of Winchester: "Thee I'll chase hence, thou wolf in sheep's array."

GREEK HISTORY

Though the Greek alphabet was developed at about the time of Homer, nobody seems to have used it to record history until the fifth century B.C. That's when Herodotus of Halicarnassus (ca. 485–425 B.C.) invented the genre of historical narrative by writing down the major events in the Greek world from the time of Croesus, king of Lydia (ca. 560 B.C.) until Xerxes' failed attempt to incorporate Greece into the Persian empire (ca. 480 B.C.). Besides being familiar with Greek literature and philosophy, Herodotus was a great traveler, and he bases much of his history on first-hand interviews.

The clash between East and West—Persia and Greece—which Herodotus depicts dominated the contemporary Hellenic world view. But even before the historian's death attention had shifted to conflicts among the Greek city-states themselves—at this time, Greece was less a country than a collection of fiercely independent regions sharing a common language and pantheon. The second great Greek historian, Thucydides (ca. 455–400 B.C.), picked up where Herodotus left off, describing and analyzing the Peloponnesian War between Athens and Sparta (431–404 B.C.). Where Herodotus is chatty and speculative, Thucydides aims at nearly scientific accuracy; but it is obvious that he took some liberties with the material (inventing speeches, for instance) in his pursuit of verisimilitude. Thucydides is nonetheless praised for his impartiality and truthfulness to fact.

The events and customs of the Greek world before Croesus and after the Peloponnesian War may be sketched in from a variety of lesser sources. The other authors I use here—such as Arrian and Plutarch—are identified in the glossary [*see* p. 211].

Oracular

The toniest shrine in Greece was doubtless that of Apollo at Delphi, situated on the slopes of Mount Parnassus, which the Greeks fancied as the center of the world. Anybody who was anybody came to Delphi to consult with the god before embarking on an important enterprise. The priestess there spent several days working herself into a trance so that she would be properly disposed to "receive" Apollo, who then considered the seeker's question and delivered a deeply obscure response.

Take for example the answer given to Athens when, threatened by the forces of the Persian king Xerxes in 480 B.C., the city sought Apollo's advice. According to the priestess, Athens was in deep trouble, but "the wooden wall only shall not fall, but help you and your children" (Herodotus, *Histories,* Book 7). Professional and amateur interpreters squabbled over what exactly Apollo had in mind, but it was finally agreed that he probably meant Athens' fleet of wooden ships. Those who thought the "wooden wall" was a thorn-hedge fencing the Acropolis (the Athenian citadel) met their doom when they retreated there as Xerxes invaded the city.

When the Romans imported the Greek practice of consultation, they called their shrines *oracula,* and thus our word "oracle," which may now mean three things: the actual place, the body of priests and priestesses that administer it, or the god's response to a question. The notorious ambiguity of these responses has inspired two more English words, "oracular" and "delphic." At first, "oracular" meant "divinely inspired" or "infallible," but had by the early eighteenth century come to mean something very different: "mysterious and inscrutable."

Laconic

The ancient Spartans have always been famous for simplicity and rigor—qualities embodied in the common English adjective "spartan." Dedicated to training fearless and courageous citizens to serve a highly regimented state, the Spartans applied to communication the same discipline they brought to military training, fostering a concise style of speech.

When, for example, Philip of Macedon wrote to the magistrates of Sparta, "If I enter Laconia, I will level Sparta to the ground," they tersely replied: "If." Laconia was the state of which Sparta was capital; thus the word "laconic" properly refers to Spartan qualities in general. But from its earliest appearances in English, "laconic" was used in particular to describe a pithy mode of discourse. Our first record of this meaning is a 1589 letter from King James VI of Scotland, later James I of England, who begs excuse for "this my laconic writing, I am in such haste." The word "laconical" appears earlier with reference to the same sort of brevity, and also with reference to an epistolary style: Abraham Fleming wrote in 1576 that "The Epistles of Nucillus were so Laconical and short"—whoever Nucillus was.

Alexander Pope kept the tradition going when he wrote in 1736, in a missive to Jonathan Swift, that "I now write no letters but of plain business, or plain how-d'ye's . . . and I grow laconic even beyond laconicism." "Laconicism" has thankfully disappeared from the language, and the briefer "laconic" survives to describe conciseness of speech rather than the difficulty of writing a respectable letter.

To Meander

Daedalus, so famous for architectural genius,
Conceived the labyrinth, which deceived the eye
With confusing signs and the winding prospects
Of manifold roundabout paths—just as
The fluid Maeander dallies through the Phrygian plains,
Flowing back and forth, errant and ambiguous.

Ovid, Metamorphoses, Book 8, lines 159–163

When you meander through a department store, you're uncon-sciously imitating the great and winding river Menderes, known to the Greeks as the Maeander. As it wends its way through the plains of western Turkey, the Maeander takes more than 600 turns, which astonished the Greeks, whose own mountainous landscape precluded so leisurely a current.

In this passage from his longish *Metamorphoses*, the Latin poet Ovid describes the construction of King Minos's labyrinth at Crete (the one with the Minotaur), which the writer compares to the winding Maeander. In fact, according to Ovid, the Maeander inspired the architect Daedalus to begin with. Whatever the merit of this fable, the Greeks applied the river's name to anything especially labyrinthine or errant, and this usage passed into our language by way of Latin.

The noun "meander," as it was first used in English, meant "a crooked course or a deceit"; Abraham Fleming wrote in 1576 of "being overwhelmed in Meanders of mischiefs." The verb "meander" appears by 1612 to name the winding of a stream, and slightly later as a metaphor of the same. Only in the nineteenth century does "meander" come to refer to the aimless wandering of a human being.

The Olympic Games

Well before the Olympic Games had an official snack food, Zeus was their official god. Held on the plain of Olympia in the Peloponnese every four years, the Olympic Games were merely one, though the most famous one, of many so-called "pan-Hellenic festivals" nominally dedicated to Greek nationalism. Hercules himself, according to legend, established the games; what is more certain is that the Olympics as we know them trace back to 776 B.C. At that time, and for a long time after, the parochial Greek city-states had a penchant for internecine warfare, from which the games offered only a brief respite. The Olympics turned out to be war continued through other means.

Each midsummer Olympian festival marked the beginning of a new "Olympiad," a period of four years used to date historical events—not just a pretentious name for the games themselves. (This book was written in the 691st Olympiad.) In any event, the games seemed to grow in scope and intensity with every Olympiad, expanding from a series of foot races to include boxing,

chariot racing, and mule-cart racing, though the last of these, thought too undignified, was later abolished. The Olympics were discontinued in the fourth century A.D., but were revived in Athens in 1896, to be interrupted only by the two world wars. At least the ancient Greeks had the sense to call a cease-fire for the games.

Draconian

The ancient Greeks considered murder a private matter in which the state had no business; it was left to the victim's family to exact justice in kind. But things took a dramatic turn in Athens in the seventh century B.C. As Herodotus and Thucydides tell the story, a proud man named Cylon, after claiming victory in the Olympic Games of 640 B.C., fancied himself just the person to rule the city-state (then controlled by the wealthiest families).

Cylon and some cronies tried to seize the Acropolis, the Athenian citadel, but failed; they then took refuge at the altar of Athena, which the city considered sacred ground. Cylon soon slipped away, but a group of his supporters remained by the altar as suppliants to the goddess. Some city magistrates finally succeeded in luring Cylon's people away from Athena's statue with promises of safe conduct, but then treacherously murdered them, even in their sacred sanctuary. Athens was shocked.

Cylon, meanwhile, fled to the neighboring state of Megara (ruled by his father-in-law) and urged an invasion of Athens. The Megarans then launched a devastating campaign. Between this external threat and the promise of a mass vendetta of blood vengeance inside Athens, things had come to a pretty pass. Something had to be done, and Athens' solution was to institute a public system of justice. Everyone involved in the disaster—Cylon, his followers, and the magistrates—was publicly tried before a jury, and all of them were exiled. A bloodbath of private retribution had thus been avoided, and the state recognized that Athens needed a more systematic legal code if such crises were to be avoided in the future.

Enter Draco, an Athenian legislator, who in 621 B.C. was given a mandate to officially codify state law. Draco's principal aim was to secure justice from the passions of private men and place it in public hands: all violations of public law were to be addressed in a public trial. Draco's code was quite an achievement—it became in fact the foundation for all Western judicial systems. Unfortunately, more famous than this achievement is the severity of his criminal penalties: a great many offenses merited death. This was just too much for Athens, which called upon the statesman Solon in the early sixth century B.C. to revise the code and to formulate a constitution.

Draco's severity is memorialized in our word "draconian," but it was also captured in a Greek proverb. Plutarch, in his *Life of Solon*, quotes the Athenian politician Demades (fourth century B.C.) as having said that "Draco wrote his laws not with ink, but with blood"—and thus our own expression "laws written in blood." "Draconian" itself does not appear in English until the late nineteenth century; but "draconic" was used by the early eighteenth century with reference to harsh laws. "Draconic" had also meant "dragon-like," as in Sir Walter Scott's *The Abbot* (1820): "'Marry come up—are you there with your bears?' muttered the dragon, with a draconic silliness" (chapter 15).

Lesbian

"Lesbian" originally meant merely "a native of the Greek island of Lesbos (new Lesvos)." But the word's present meaning derives from one particular resident, the poet Sappho (b. ca. 612 B.C.). As a girl, she was initiated into a cult of Aphrodite and the Muses—patrons of love and the arts, respectively. This intimate group of young women inspired Sappho's first poems, which celebrate the girls' close friendship and their marriages—Sappho herself later married a man named Cercylas.

What is remarkable about her poetry, besides its quality, is its celebration of close and emotionally rich female relationships—only her brother and her son inspire as much warmth. Sappho's frank preference for women's society lies behind our use of the word "lesbian," though there's no evidence of her sexual involvement with other members of the cult. (On the other hand, the Greeks thought of Lesbos as a particularly wanton locale.) Later writers even concocted the story that Sappho, after the failure of a love affair with the ferryman Phaon, threw herself off a cliff.

Despite the rich and contradictory lore surrounding Sappho's life, the word "lesbian" was for centuries put to merely prosaic uses, primarily in such phrases as "lesbian rule" and "lesbian square." Aristotle describes the lesbian rule, in his *Nicomachean Ethics*, as a leaden ruler that "adapts itself to the shape of the stone and is not rigid." When Samuel Daniel introduced the word "lesbian" to English in 1601, he was referring to the lesbian rule, which came to serve as a metaphor for an adaptable set of principles. This usage virtually disappeared after the eighteenth century.

"Lesbianism" meaning "female homosexuality" is first recorded in an 1870 diary entry by A. J. Munby, who reports that the poet Swinburne "expressed a horror of sodomy . . . and an actual admiration of Lesbianism, being unable . . . to see that that is equally loathsome." Subsequent uses of "lesbianism" and "lesbian" are even more pejorative, until about the 1970s. C. Day Lewis, for example, claimed in 1936 that women never write real poetry, "unless they're invalids or Lesbians or something." I suspect that Sappho would have had something to say to that.

A Mausoleum

Mausolus, the eldest son of Hecatomnus, married Artemisia, the elder daughter; Hidrieus, the second son, married Ada, the other sister. Mausolus came to the throne, and, dying without children, left the kingdom to his wife, by whom the above-mentioned sepulchre was erected. She pined away for grief at the loss of her husband.

Strabo, *Geography*, Book 14, chapter 2

When the handsome King Mausolus of Caria (now southwestern Turkey) died in 353 B.C., his wife Artemisia was beside herself. Not only had she lost a husband, she had also lost a brother—such was the wisdom of their father, the previous king, to keep the crown firmly in the family. After Mausolus's body was burned, Artemisia mixed the ashes in liquor and drank the stuff up, which may have inspired her to build, according to the late king's plan, an obscenely expensive and ostentatious monument in his memory.

Artemisia employed four architects—one for each side of the building—and then retained a fifth to erect a pyramid on top. Huge statues of the queen and former king (the latter now housed in the British Museum) were placed within the structure, which was about 250 feet to the side and 135 feet high. The building took so long to complete that Artemisia died in the meantime. But when finished it became esteemed as one of the wonders of the ancient world, and was known as *Mausoleion* in Greek, in honor of Mausolus. The structure is supposed to have been toppled either by an earthquake or by the Crusaders in the middle ages; its ruins were excavated in the 1850s.

From the Greek *Mausoleion* came the English "mausoleum," first recorded in the 1540s. By 1600, "mausoleum" had come to refer to any commemorative burial place.

A Colossus

The Greek word *colossos* seems to have first appeared in the writings of the historian Herodotus (fifth century B.C.), who refers to gigantic Egyptian statues. Subsequently *colossos* was used to describe one particular statue, a 70-cubit (100-foot) bronze representation of the god Apollo on the Greek island of Rhodes. The Rhodians built this colossus—which is supposed, though the evidence is against it, to have straddled the entrance to their main harbor—to celebrate their victory over the Macedonian king Antigonus I in 306 B.C.

The Colossus of Rhodes, as it is now known, is regarded as one of the wonders of the ancient world [*see* p. 209]. It was twelve years in the making, and was built well enough to survive unperturbed for the better part of a century. An earthquake in 224 B.C. inflicted severe damage, however, and for about nine centuries the Colossus stood in its pitiful state, despite the attempts of benefactors to get the Rhodians to repair it. According to some accounts, the statue was finally sold in A.D. 672 by the island's Arabic rulers to a merchant of Edessa (now Urfa, Turkey), who carted it off piecemeal on 900 camels.

The word "colossus" was first used in English in the late fourteenth century, when John de Trevisa translated a report that "In this city of Rodus was a colossus of brass seventy cubits high, and in this same isle . . . were an hundred less Colossus." Later, Shakespeare has the envious Cassius fume that Julius Caesar "doth bestride the narrow world/ Like a Colossus" (*Julius Caesar*, Act 1, scene 2). Since the late eighteenth century, we've put Rhodes to the side and used "colossus" as a common noun for anything really big.

Call No Man Happy until He Dies

"Many of the wealthiest men have been unfortunate, and many of modest means have had excellent luck. . . . The wealthy man can better satisfy his desires and bear sudden calamity; the poor man, though less able to withstand evils, may be kept clear of them by good luck, and furthermore he enjoys many blessings: he is whole of limb, a stranger to disease, free from misfortune, happy in his children, and beautiful to look on. If, in addition, he ends his life well, he is truly the man you're looking for, the man who may rightly be called happy. But call no man happy until he dies; rather, call him fortunate."

Herodotus, *Histories*, Book 1, chapter 32

To call the Greeks fatalistic would be an understatement. So the Lydian king Croesus (560–546 B.C.) should have known better than to ask the Athenian lawgiver Solon who he thought was the happiest man alive. Croesus, very wealthy and thus very vain [*see* RICH AS CROESUS], is obviously fishing for compliments, expecting Solon to answer "Croesus, of course." Solon, however, first names an obscure Athenian whose happiness lay mostly in his heroic death.

Croesus, taken aback, then asks who the *second* happiest man is; but once again Solon refuses to cooperate, naming two young men of Argos whose deaths seemed heaven-sent. Perhaps you're starting to get the picture: in Solon's opinion, life is at best a chancy proposition, and your fortunes are liable to turn at any moment. But if you happen to die nobly after living a trouble-free life, well, *then* you've earned the right to be called happy.

Croesus thinks Solon a fool; if what you possess now doesn't make you happy, what good is life? But subsequent events change Croesus's mind—Herodotus thinks the gods want to teach him a lesson. First, one of the king's sons is killed while hunting; two years later, his kingdom is overthrown by the Persians, and he is taken captive. The Persian king Cyrus then orders Croesus to be thrown into a pyre, and Croesus, facing his end, remembers what Solon had told him. As the bitter truth dawns on him, Croesus, in anguish, utters Solon's name. Well, one thing leads to another, as the curious Cyrus asks who this "Solon" is, and is moved by Croesus's story. Cyrus spares him, and the two become bosom buddies. (Remember this story—it could save your life one day.)

Solon's aphorism echoes a line from Aeschylus's tragedy *Agamemnon*: "Call that man only blest/ who has in sweet tranquility brought his life to a close" (lines 928–929); and the idea later surfaces in the last lines of Sophocles' *Oedipus the King*: "Count no mortal happy till/ he has passed the final limit of his life secure from pain." Aristotle, too, endorses the idea in his *Ethics*. This very Greek idea first appears in English in John Florio's 1603 translation of Montaigne's essays.

Rich as Croesus

> Croesus, resolving to propitiate the Delphic god with a magnificent sacrifice, offered up three thousand of every kind of sacrificial beast; he also made a huge pile of couches overlaid with silver and gold, golden goblets, and robes of velvet and purple, all of which he burned in hopes of securing the god's favor. . . . When the sacrifice was ended, the king melted down a vast quantity of gold into 117 ingots, making them six palms long, three palms broad, and one palm in thickness.
>
> Herodotus, *Histories*, Book 1, chapter 50

And so forth—the list goes on for quite a while. Just how rich was Croesus? By my calculation, the gold ingots alone, which weigh a combined total of 13,450 pounds, would be worth about $84 million in 1990 U.S. dollars. This accounts for a fraction of Croesus's offerings to the god Apollo, whose oracle at Delphi offers critical advice as Croesus prepares for war with Persia. Unfortunately, Croesus grows too confident in his reading of the oracle, and ultimately meets with disaster [*see* p. 43].

By Herodotus's time, the wealth of Croesus was a well-established legend, inspiring even the Greeks' imaginations—despite the fact that Croesus mounted the first serious threat to their freedom. In later times, the phrase "as rich as Croesus"—found in English by the sixteenth century—became more famous than Croesus (pronounced "creases") himself. Which is why one character in William Thackeray's novel *The History of Pendennis* (1850) describes another with the blunder "as rich as Crazes." More creative is Bertie Wooster's substitution in P. G. Wodehouse's "Jeeves Makes an Omelette"—he calls one of his uncles "as rich as creosote."

A Marathon

Before they left the city, the Athenian generals sent off to Sparta a herald, one Pheidippides, by birth an Athenian and by profession and practice a trained runner. . . . Pheidippides reached Sparta the very next day, and went before the rulers to say: "Men of Lacedaemon, the Athenians beg you to hasten to their aid, and not to allow their state, the most ancient in all Greece, to be enslaved by the barbarians."

Herodotus, *Histories*, Book 6, chapters 105–106

In 490 B.C., the Persian king Darius threatened to invade Athens, landing his forces at Marathon, a coastal city in Athens' province. Athens quickly dispatched a force to meet them; they also sent the famous runner Pheidippides to Sparta with a plea for help. Amazingly, Pheidippides accomplished the journey—about 75 miles by land—in one day. Unfortunately, the Spartans were not so swift in mobilizing a backup force, but the Athenians managed to fend off the Persians without them.

After the success at Marathon, the Athenians sent out another runner to take home the news of their victory. Though he had only 25 miles to go this time, it is said that he ran so fast that after delivering his message he dropped dead. By some modern accounts, this second runner was Pheidippides himself, but the identification lacks classical authority. Fact or fiction, the legend inspired the Greeks, as they revived the Olympic Games in 1896 [*see* p. 36], to institute a 25-mile race (later 26.2 miles) named after the battle of Marathon.

Ostracism

These days you might be ostracized for such crimes as wearing the wrong clothes or being born with the wrong surname. But in the fifth century B.C. in Athens, ostracism was a legal procedure invented to punish political indiscretion. The reformer Cleisthenes, founder of Athenian democracy, designed a new political system intended to respond, more or less, to the will of the people, and he was not about to have any of the old aristocrats mess things up. Each year, an assembly of all citizens would decide whether anyone had earned expulsion from the state for being a menace—a process that eventually devolved into an unpopularity contest. Citizens voted for their favorite public enemy by inscribing his name on a fragment of pottery, in Greek an *ostrakon*. Winners were promptly banished from the city for ten years. In the seventy-year history of Athenian ostracism, about ten men suffered this fate.

The procedure is first mentioned in English literature by Sir Thomas North in his 1580 translation of Plutarch, but he calls it "Ostracismon" after the actual Greek term. Romancer and pamphleteer Robert Greene introduced the modern spelling in 1588 while recommending a cure that would be "as sure a repulse to melancholy, as the *Ostracism* was to the noble of Athens." In the early seventeenth century John Donne first used "ostracism" as a common noun meaning "banishment," and fellow poet Andrew Marvell later coined the verb "ostracize."

The Greek *ostrakon*, in addition to meaning "potsherd," also meant "hard shell," and thus the word "ostracize" is crowded in dictionaries by a long list of zoological coinages, such as "ostreaceous" ("oyster-like") and "ostracoid" ("shell-like").

If You Want Peace, Prepare for War

"Acknowledging then, allies, that there is no alternative, and that we are advising you for the best, vote for war; be not afraid of the immediate danger, but fix your thoughts on the durable peace which will follow. For by war peace is assured, but to remain at peace when you should be going to war may prove very dangerous."

Thucydides, *History of the Peloponnesian War*, Book 1, chapter 124

The situation in Greece in 442 B.C. was increasingly perilous, as Athens consolidated an alliance of city-states and made little secret of its more ambitious designs. Sparta, feeling the pinch, called a congress to decide how its own alliance should respond to Athenian aggression.

Thucydides rehearses the speech of Corinth's representative, who pretty much preaches to the converted—the prevailing sentiment was already for war. The Corinthian eloquently argues that avoiding war is the surest way to surrender peace— that is, security and freedom. War is coming nonetheless, since Athens will not voluntarily desist from its imperial aggression; the best course of action is thus to nip its designs in the bud.

The Corinthian's argument was widely quoted in the classical world. An English equivalent appeared by the 1530s, and later became one of George Washington's favorite sayings. On January 8, 1790, for example, he asserted to the United States Congress that "To be prepared for war is one of the most effective ways of preserving peace." Theodore Roosevelt echoed his predecessor in 1897, when, as Assistant Secretary of State, he told those assembled at the Naval War College that "Again and again we have owed peace to the fact that we were prepared for war." The argument was tirelessly repeated during the U.S. congressional debate, in January 1991, over authorizing the use of force in Iraq.

To Smell of the Lamp

If it happened that Demosthenes attended any lengthy speech, he would repeat it to himself, embellishing and revising it; he likewise altered any matter he heard or rehearsed to others. Therefore men arrived at the opinion that he was not naturally endowed with wit, nor was his eloquence natural, but rather artificially acquired by extreme labor. . . . Once, Pytheas, taunting Demosthenes, told him his reasons smelled of the lamp. "Yes," Demosthenes sharply replied, "but there is a great difference, Pytheas, between your labor by lamplight and mine."

Plutarch, *Life of Demosthenes*, paragraph 8

Once the famous Greek orator and lawyer Demosthenes (384–322 B.C.) learns the value of practice, he becomes a little obsessive about it. Most people know the stories of his declaiming with a mouth full of stones and of his shouting against the waves; Plutarch tells the more revealing tale of how Demosthenes, in an attempt to force himself to spend more time practicing in his study, shaved one side of his head so that shame, if nothing else, would prevent his venturing out.

Whether or not any of these tales is true, Demosthenes, once a weak speaker, clearly profited from his studies, though they didn't much improve his extempore performances. In fact, he became notorious for a defect of spontaneity and an excess of pedantry. Furthermore, when called upon to make a political speech, he refused to satisfy the people unless he were already prepared to address the topic. The popular Athenian leader Pytheas goads Demosthenes for this, telling him his arguments "smelled of the lamp"—in other words, that they smack too much of study. (Compare the modern expression "to burn the midnight oil.") Demosthenes in turn insinuates that if Pytheas burns the lamp, it isn't because he's studying anything.

Pytheas's phrase is more famous than Demosthenes' comeback, and justly so. Erasmus recorded the insult in his book of adages, which was translated into English in 1542—though the translator renders the phrase as "smelled of the candle." Michel de Montaigne, a champion of spontaneity, alludes to the incident in one of his essays, whose English translation (1603) comes closer to the familiar version: "We commonly say of some compositions, that they smell of the oil, and of the lamp, by reason of a certain harshness, and rudeness, which long plodding labor imprints in them that be much elaborated" ("Of Ready or Slow Speech"). Francis Bacon established the final form of the phrase when he reported in 1605 that "Aeschines" (his mistake for Pytheas) told Demosthenes "that his orations did smell of the lamp."

A Gordian Knot

It was said of Gordius's wagon that whoever could loosen the knot of the yoke was destined to rule Asia. The cord was made of cornel bark, and neither end nor beginning to it could be seen. Some say that when Alexander could find no way to loosen the cord and yet was unwilling to allow it to remain knotted, lest this should exercise some disturbing influence upon the multitude, he struck it with his sword, cutting it through, and proclaimed that it had been loosened. . . . Both he and his troops left the wagon as if the oracular prediction concerning the loosening of the knot had been duly fulfilled.

Arrian, *Anabasis of Alexander,* Book 2, chapter 3

In the middle of his campaign against Persia, around 333 B.C., Alexander the Great makes a stop in the Phrygian capital of Gordium, not far from the present Turkish capital Ankara. Among Gordium's attractions is an old chariot that, according to the legend, once belonged to Gordius, a peasant who became king of Phrygia in about the eighth century B.C., and whose son Midas was later bestowed with a golden touch. The legend also had it that Zeus sent to Gordius an eagle that alighted on the chariot's yoke; the knot of this yoke was thus thought to embody imperial power, and an oracle declared that whoever could untie it would rule all of Asia.

Enter Alexander, whose ambition and vanity would never permit him to leave Gordium without somehow untying that knot. When he was stymied in the attempt, his impatience moved him to draw his sword and hack the thing to pieces. Not a very imaginative move, perhaps; but no one had dared do such a thing before, so Alexander's audacity was clearly something Asia would have to reckon with. And in any case, the gods apparently assented to Alexander's unorthodox means of fulfilling the oracle, since they thundered their approval and eventually helped him conquer all of Asia—which in Alexander's day extended only as far as India.

The story of the Gordian knot passed from legend into proverb, and "to cut the Gordian knot" came to mean "to solve a problem by sheer force or by trampling on the rules." Sometimes, however, we use "Gordian knot" to mean "a difficult problem" without reference to Alexander's petulant solution. About a decade after the phrase first appears in English, for example, Shakespeare has the Archbishop of Canterbury describe King Henry the Fifth as one who, presented with political conundrum, "The Gordian knot of it he will unloose,/ Familiar as his garter" (*King Henry the Fifth*, Act 1, scene 1). We assume the king does not remove his garter by hacking it to pieces.

GREEK PHILOSOPHY

We tend to think of Greek philosophy as the invention and property of Socrates, Plato, and Aristotle; yet while it is true that they are its towering figures, the Greeks had been toying with systems of philosophical thought for at least two centuries before Socrates. The ideas of the "Pre-Socratics," as they're known, survive only in fragments and quotations, but it is nonetheless possible to piece together from these their basic notions about the gods and the universe.

Fields that we now consider sciences—astronomy, physics, mathematics, and biology—all originated in the questioning and theorizing of Greek and Arabic philosophers. The first recognized Greek philosopher, Thales of Miletus (sixth century B.C.), for example, practically invented geometry and physics by adapting Egyptian methods of measuring shapes and by theorizing on the composition of matter (he thought everything was composed of water). Later, Pythagoras (ca. 572–500 B.C.), by attempting to interpret the whole world in terms of numbers, inspired the mathematical mania for reducing everything to formulas and equations.

By the time of Socrates (469–399 B.C.), when the hub of Greek philosophy moved to Athens, philosophy had become a sort of profession, with its own schools, exemplified by a group of philosophers-for-hire known as the Sophists [*see* p. 75]. The Sophists' competitors responded in kind, establishing their own schools and having their teachings recorded for posterity. I will deal with the two great writers of this period—Plato and Aristotle—in their own sections. Phrases derived from other post-Socratic philosophers are included here.

Art Is Long, Life Is Short

Life is short, art is long, the occasion fleeting, experiment fallacious, judgment difficult. The physician must not only be prepared to do what is right himself, but also to make the patient, the attendants, and the externals cooperate.

Hippocrates, *Aphorisms*, section 1

Hippocrates' *Aphorisms*, written or collected circa 415 B.C., used to be the most famous of the seventy-two works on medicine attributed to him; it was even referred to as "the physicians' Bible" until the nineteenth century. And still famous is the very first aphorism, remembered by its opening words: "Life is short, art is long." This phrase, however, means something very different now than in the original. Hippocrates could mean two things: "our life is short, and the art of medicine takes long to learn; it is a pursuit fraught with peril and difficulty"; or, more probably, "the practice of medicine is full of uncertainty and delay, and hesitant treatment may ensure that the patient's life is a short one." A good physician must seize the moment and bend it to the patient's present needs. In either case, we now mean something more sentimental, such as "great works of art are enduring though the artist's life is fleeting."

Seneca's Latin version of the phrase—*vita brevis, ars longa*—is almost as recognizable as the English and certainly more famous than Hippocrates' Greek. The romantic English version was perhaps established by Longfellow, who writes, in *A Psalm of Life* (1839): "Art is long, and Time is fleeting." In other words, "Lives of great men all remind us/ We can make our lives sublime,/ And, departing, leave behind us/ Footprints on the sands of time."

A Cynic

Nobody likes being called a cynic. And the insult is further compounded when you realize that it's the Greek equivalent of being called a dog. What we mean by the word today is in fact a bit remote from what the Athenians meant when they called the disciples of Antisthenes "cynics." Antisthenes, a student of Socrates, set up philosophical shop in a gymnasium outside Athens, where he preached the primacy of virtue and the worthlessness of material things. Happiness, in his view, has nothing to do with pleasure or gain, but rather with freedom from desires and purity of soul. Antisthenes attracted his share of pupils, notably Diogenes [*see* DIOGENES' TUB], but most Athenians found the lot of them self-satisfied and self-righteous.

The gymnasium where Antisthenes taught was called Cynosarges, which, happily enough for the philosopher's detractors, resembles the Greek word for "dog-like": *cynikos*. Thus the nickname "cynic," which conveyed the appropriate amount of contempt for people who were not overly concerned with personal hygiene, and whose ascetic ways placed them outside what passed for civil society. (Diogenes himself made sardonic fun of the nickname; when asked what he had done to be called a dog, he replied: "I fawn on those who give me anything, I yelp at those who refuse, and I set my teeth in rascals.")

Given this history, it is easier to understand what Englishmen meant when they began using the words "cynic" and "cynical" in the sixteenth century. In Robert Greene's 1588 romance *Pandosto*, a frustrated lover asks, "Canst thou not love? Cometh this cynical passion of prone desires, or peevish frowardness [perversity]?"—in other words, "do you scorn love because your heart is cold, or because you're stubborn?" In the anonymous play *The Pilgrimage to Parnassus* (1597), one character protests that "I am not such a piece of cynic earth/ That I neglect sweet beauty's delight" (Act 4, line 468). The phrase "snarling cynics" was a favorite of the satirist John Marston, and it takes care of etymology even as it captures the cynic's disdain.

The cynics' haughtiness and contempt of comfort soon became associated with a sneering attitude toward humanity in general; and the modern sense of "cynical"—"disposed to devalue people's motives"—emerged by the nineteenth century. Oscar Wilde supplied this nice definition in his play *Lady Windermere's Fan* (1892): "What is a cynic?—a person who knows the price of everything and the value of nothing." George Meredith observed in *The Egoist* (1879) that "Cynics are only happy in making the world as barren to others as they have made it for themselves." Well, that's a little cynical, don't you think?

Diogenes' Tub

"O foolishness of men! that . . . fetch their precepts from the Cynic tub,/ Praising the lean and sallow Abstinence." So exclaims the demigod Comus, in John Milton's *Masque Presented at Ludlow Castle* (1634). But what does abstinence have to do with a tub, and what does a tub have to do with cynicism?

Diogenes of Sinope was the most die-hard adherent of Antisthenes the cynic [*see* p. 55], who preached denial of the flesh. According to legend, Diogenes was so contemptuous of the easy life that he chose to inhabit an earthenware tub in an Athenian temple—lodgings equivalent to the typical New York studio today. Diogenes was, as John Brown put it in 1751, "the unbred cynic snarling in his tub" ("cynic" means "dog-like" in Greek). Such ostentatious asceticism and indifference to opinion became identified with the cynic doctrine, and Diogenes' tub has become a metaphor for the misanthrope's retreat. Diogenes has also lent his name to the Diogenes crab, a denizen of the West Indies that makes its home in empty shells.

Plutarch (among others), in his *Life of Alexander the Great,* relates the most famous legend of Diogenes. Alexander, proclaimed general of all Greece, is visited at Corinth by various philosophers and dignitaries, but not by the famous Diogenes. The general ventures forth to find the cynic, and discovers him sunbathing. When Alexander asks whether there were anything he might do for Diogenes, the latter replies, "stand out of my sun a little." Alexander greatly marveled at Diogenes' boldness; "if I were not Alexander," he rhapsodized, "I would be Diogenes."

Eclectic

One more school of philosophy was introduced not long ago by Potamon of Alexandria, who chose from each of the others what pleased him: this is the Eclectic sect.

Diogenes Laertius, *Lives of Eminent Philosophers*, Book 1, prologue

Though Diogenes Laertius is writing in the third century A.D., it seems that Potamon, founder of the Eclectic school, was a slightly older contemporary of the Roman emperor Augustus, who ruled from 43 B.C. to A.D. 14. This was an exciting time in Alexandria, where Greeks, Romans, Jews, and Egyptians mingled and debated; cultures crossed, and ideas combined. Potamon himself set about to reconcile the Academic and Peripatetic philosophies [*see* pp. 85 and 103] with the Roman version of Stoicism [*see* p. 78]. He called the result "eclectic," from the Greek *eklektikos*, "selecting."

The technique of eclecticism involves selecting from a variety of philosophical systems those elements that can be fit together in a larger, more inclusive system. This process by necessity excludes what is most individual—and often what is most powerful—in the original systems, which is why it has earned the scorn of most philosophers from Potamon's day to our own. Nonetheless, eclecticism saw a revival in nineteenth-century France, where it was spearheaded by Victor Cousin, who combined the ideas of various contemporary French, Scottish, and German schools.

The term "eclectic" first entered English as a philosophical term. By the mid-nineteenth century, "eclectic" had begun to take on its vaguer modern meaning of "borrowing opinions, tastes, ideas, or styles from a variety of sources."

Epicurean

The way we toss about the words "epicure" and "epicurean" can sometimes be very confusing. Generally, we praise the epicure's refined tastes, and denounce the epicurean's hedonism and gluttony [*see* HEDONISM]. The confusion arises from different views of the life and teachings of the Athenian philosopher Epicurus (341–270 B.C.), who left behind him a collection of maxims as well as a number of legends.

Basically, Epicurus counseled avoiding superstition and pursuing pleasure. Since he put no stock in tales of the gods and saw no evidence of divine intervention in daily life, he concluded that what is good depends on what strikes the senses as good: man, in effect, is the measure of all things [*see* p. 89]. Pleasure is thus the ultimate good, and pain the ultimate evil.

But Epicurus hardly advocated debauchery, since he also taught that what seems pleasurable on the surface—sex, for example—often conceals a great deal of trouble. And while it is good to satisfy our natural desires for food and drink, overindulgence leads to gas pains, hangovers, and other disturbances.

Desires for fine clothes and gourmet food, furthermore, are simply vain. By pleasure Epicurus meant the simple pleasure which leads to ease of mind.

How we got to "epicure" and "epicurean" from here is a matter of how Epicurus's followers interpreted his teachings. The Romans are the villains of this tale: they took Epicurus's philosophy of pleasure—which basically meant absence of pain—and turned it into a philosophy of unthinking indulgence. At first, Epicurus's name was used by English writers with reference to his scorn of superstitious tales. As one moralist complained in 1589, "The school of Epicure, and the Atheists, is mightily increased these days." Soon thereafter, however, "epicure" came to refer to a devotee of sensual gratification, and at the same time to someone who has cultivated a palate worthy of it.

But these two latter senses have parted ways. "Epicurean" retains the derogatory sense expressed by John Smith in 1652: "These poor brutish Epicureans have nothing but the mere husks of fleshly pleasure to feed themselves with." The "epicure," on the other hand, fares a little better, as in Sir Walter Scott's description of how the "epicure protracts, by sipping slowly, the enjoyment of a delicious beverage" (*Waverly*, 1814).

Eureka!

According to the story, Archimedes, as he was washing, thought of a way to compute the proportion of gold in King Hieron's crown by observing how much water flowed over the bathing-stool. He leapt up as one possessed, crying *heureka!* ("I've found it!"). After repeating this several times, he went his way. But, among the many millions of dissolute debauchees that both this and the preceding ages have produced, we never yet heard of a glutton that exclaimed with such vehemence, "I've eaten!" or of an amorous gallant that ever cried "I've kissed!"

Plutarch, "The Impossibility of Pleasure according to Epicurus"

You may be surprised to discover that "eureka!" derives from the simple Greek verb *heuriskein,* "to find"—*heureka* means "I have found it." But the great mathematician Archimedes (ca. 287–212 B.C.) instantly transformed this common expression into an untranslatable cry of triumph. It would be like shouting out "I bought it!" today and having some forty-third-century Frenchman quote your English whenever he struck a particularly good bargain.

What inspired Archimedes was his discovery, as he sloshed about in his bathwater, of hydrostatics, the science of the behavior of solid bodies in liquids. Simply put, he could tell his friend King Hieron II of Syracuse whether the gold in his crown had been alloyed with a base metal by throwing it in a bathtub: the weight of water it displaced would reveal its specific gravity and thus its composition.

English quotations of Archimedes trace back to 1570, about thirty years before the first translation of Plutarch's account. The expression came into its own during the eighteenth century, and a little later "eureka" was adapted to hawking products— "Eureka shirts," for example, were advertised in *Atheneum* magazine in 1853. This was about five years after the California Gold Rush, which later lent the motto "Eureka!" to a state now famous for its hot-tubs. (No crowns, however, are known to have been fashioned from California gold.) Coincidentally, Ronald Reagan, who would later become governor of California (among other things), attended Eureka College—which is not in Eureka, California, but Eureka, Illinois.

Today, "eureka" is not just a bray of self-congratulation and a state motto, it's also the proprietary name of a particular alloy of copper and nickel used in filaments and electrical wire. Throw a lightbulb in the bathtub, and you'll discover there's not a trace of gold in it.

When Archimedes wasn't playing in his tub, he laid the foundations for calculus, invented the "Archimedean screw" (an hydraulic lifting device), attempted to calculate the number of grains of sand it would take to fill the universe, approximated the value of π, and derived the theory of the lever. Quite pleased with himself over the last of these achievements, Archimedes

boasted, "Give me a place to stand, and I will move the earth." He might have contented himself with building a lever to lift a battleship, since if the lever were long enough and the fulcrum close enough to the ship, that would be possible (he did in fact drag a loaded ship with pulleys).

Hedonism

In the second edition of his *Confessions of an English Opium Eater* (1856), Thomas De Quincey attributes the invention of the word "hedonist" to a certain Professor Wilson, who at one point announces, "Gentlemen, I am a *Hedonist;* and if you *must* know why I take opium, that's the reason why." If the professor's auditors were confused by this new word, they could have turned to the English translation, published the same year, of *Schwegler's History of Philosophy*, which defines hedonism as "the philosophical doctrine of the Cyreneans that pleasure is the chief good."

The "Cyreneans," or Cyrenaics, were followers of the Greek philosopher Aristippus (fourth century B.C.), a pupil of Socrates who later taught at Cyrene. Though none of Aristippus's works survive, it is thought that he (or perhaps his grandson, also named Aristippus) championed pleasure as the consummate good. This creed is aptly called "hedonism" since *hedone* is Greek for pleasure, and it gave rise in the seventeenth century to the English word "hedonic," meaning "pleasurable" or "pleasure-seeking."

Like the teachings of his spiritual heir Epicurus [*see* p. 59], Aristippus's hedonism has earned a bad rap over the years. He himself warned that not all pleasures are good for you, and some of them actually lead to pain. One must therefore be wise in seeking pleasure. Before Professor Wilson confessed to his hedonistic habit, the philosopher Jeremy Bentham asserted that pleasure-seeking is all to the good, as long as one seeks pleasure for others as well. Bentham, to use his own words, advocated "the greatest amount of happiness for the greatest number." A far cry from the aim of today's hedonist, whose self-centered "me me me" lifestyle mocks the truly hedonistic attitude.

The Hippocratic Oath

I swear by Apollo Physician, and Asclepius, and Health, and Panacea, and all the gods and goddesses, that according to my ability and judgment I will keep this Oath and this stipulation. . . . I will use whatever treatment that, according to my ability and judgment, I consider beneficial to my patients, and abstain from whatever is deleterious and mischievous. I will give no deadly medicine to anyone when asked, nor suggest any such counsel; likewise I will not give to any woman a contraceptive to produce abortion. With purity and holiness I will pass my life and practice my Art.

Hippocrates, "Oath," excerpt

Who devised this oath, and when, we cannot know for sure, but it is traditionally ascribed to the Greek physician Hippocrates (ca. 460–377 B.C.), and it has made his name a household word. About all we know of the man is that he was short and fond of travel; Plato adds that he believed the human body to be a unified whole whose parts worked together organically—a novel idea at the time. Plato also notes that he accepted fees for his services, thus pioneering a grand medical tradition.

Hippocrates' Oath is based on a belief that life is sacred, and that the physician is morally bound to protect it in all circumstances. These core ideas are about all that survive of the oath, which in modern form is still administered to most graduates of medical school. (The outmoded passages were edited out in 1948 by the World Medical Association.) Young doctors no longer swear by Apollo Physician, Asclepius, and the rest—Apollo being the Greek god of the professions among other things, and Apollo's son Asclepius being the god of healing. References to specific procedures have also been dropped—not only the forbidding of poisoning and abortion, but also the strictures on gossiping and on surgery, which was to be left to trained craftsmen. There is no mention of whether such craftsmen were required to take out malpractice insurance.

Know Thyself

> I judge that man
> Despicable, who knows how much higher is Atlas
> Than all the mountains in Libya, yet at the same time
> Is ignorant of how unlike an iron box is to a purse.
> From the heavens descends "know thyself" [*gnothi seauton*];
> It should be fixed upon the mind and wielded by the memory,
> Whether you seek a wife or desire a seat in the senate.
>
> Juvenal, "Eleventh Satire," lines 22–26

The Roman satirist Juvenal, laughing at people who pride themselves on their useless knowledge and meager talents, hauls out a truly ancient piece of advice: "Know thyself." As he puts it later, "Take your own measure and keep it in mind, in great matters or small ones." In other words, don't try to spend more than you have: know your own limits and pursue what you're actually capable of.

Juvenal quotes the phrase "Know thyself" in its original Greek form, which was passed down among the sayings of the Seven Sages of Greece [*see* p. 72]. This particular phrase was traditionally attributed to Thales, who established the first Greek philosophical school at Miletus. However, since Thales left no writings, it's hard to be sure whether he coined the hoary proverb or not; other Sages sometimes get the credit, as does Socrates. But in Plato's *Protagoras* Socrates himself cites the wise men, explaining that these sages "met together and dedicated in the temple of Apollo at Delphi, as the first fruits of their wisdom, the far-famed inscriptions, which are in all men's mouths, 'Know thyself' and 'Nothing too much.'" Whether or not this is how the phrase got inscribed on the oracle, it later became its most famous piece of advice [*see* ORACULAR *and* NOTHING IN EXCESS].

Juvenal understood this wise saying in a practical sense, but after it was introduced into English, by Sir Thomas Elyot in

1531, it gradually became freighted with spiritual meaning. It was no longer good enough merely to assess your capabilities; to know yourself meant delving into the recesses of your soul. The narrator of Thomas Carlyle's *Sartor Resartus* (1833–1834) objected, however, calling "know thyself" in this sense an "impossible precept" which might "be translated into this partially possible one, 'Know what thou canst work at.'" Juvenal would have agreed.

To Live According to Nature

Epicurus also said: "If you live according to nature, you will never be poor; but if according to opinions, you will never be rich." Nature demands little, opinion a great deal.

Seneca the Younger, *Moral Epistles*, epistle 16

Confronted with the many contradictions between the writings and the life of the Roman politician, dramatist, and philosopher Seneca the Younger (ca. 4 B.C.–A.D. 65), the scholar E. Phillips Barker concludes that "Seneca's life and works present a fairly clear-cut picture of neurosis." The estimation of earlier generations was more generous; Seneca was esteemed the quintessential Stoic, and his tragedies were the ultimate basis for Renaissance works in the genre. Perhaps Seneca's Stoicism was a neurotic flight from reality; perhaps not. In any case, in the letter excerpted here he shows that he learned much from Epicurus as well as from Zeno [*see* STOIC]. (He perhaps also read his Horace—*see* IF YOU CAST OUT NATURE WITH A FORK, IT WILL STILL RETURN.)

According to the fragmentary evidence, confirmed by Seneca's report, Epicurus held that one should "live according to nature." He did not mean, as we do, that you should retire to the country, eat roots, and cooperate with the ecosystem. Rather, he meant that you should listen when your body says "stop." True Epicureanism is learning the natural limits of pleasure [*see* p. 59]. But opinion, by which Epicurus meant "the lessons of the crowd," leads you to always seek more than is natural. For example, says Seneca, what do riches teach the average man but to seek more riches? Opinion has it that you can never be too wealthy, but immoderate desire for gain is unnatural and ultimately painful, since it can never be satisfied.

As it turns out, Seneca was himself quite a rich man, and he was not exactly embarrassed by his own pursuit of greater wealth. Furthermore, even as he retailed moral instruction in his letters, he was conspicuously amoral when it came to public "service"—Seneca could flatter and abet whoever was in power with the best of them. It was perhaps not very "natural," for example, when Seneca helped Nero murder the emperor's own mother in A.D. 59. It was only a matter of time before Nero turned on his lackey, at which point Seneca decided he could no longer live, either according to nature or according to opinion, and he took his own life.

Nature Abhors a Vacuum

All the natural philosophers from Thales to Plato rejected a vacuum. Empedocles says that there is nothing of a vacuity in nature, nor any thing superabundant. Leucippus, Democritus, Demetrius, Metrodorus, Epicurus, that the atoms are infinite in number; and that a vacuum is infinite in magnitude. The Stoics, that within the compass of the world there is no vacuum, but beyond it the vacuum is infinite. Aristotle that the vacuum beyond the world is so great that the heaven has liberty to breathe into it, for the heaven is fiery.

Plutarch, Maxims of the Philosophers, Book 1, Chapter 18

Empedocles (484–424 B.C.) was best known to later writers for his theory that the universe is composed of four elements (earth, air, fire, and water) and governed by two contrary forces, Love and Strife [*see* HARMONY IN DISCORD]. But today, outside universities, another of his ideas is much more familiar: that "nature abhors a vacuum." Empedocles himself said that "No part of the All is empty, nor too full"; he reasons that if there were an emptiness somewhere, "whence, then, could anything come into being?"

The logic of this escapes me—how would a vacuum elsewhere preclude generation here?—but perhaps Empedocles' idea is that natural generation requires an unlimited source of fresh material, so that the universe itself must be completely "full." Aristotle reports and ridicules this theory in *On the Heavens*, but he takes issue with Empedocles' logic rather than with his denial that a vacuum or "void" can exist in nature. Plutarch's account of Aristotle's theory is thus mistaken. In fact, Aristotle, who became the champion of later nay-sayers, argues in the *Physics* (Book 4) that the presumption of a "void" leads to conclusions which contradict the laws of motion and violate our experience of space.

Empedocles does not actually say in so many words that "nature abhors a vacuum," though he implies as much. The exact phrase first appears, in Latin, in François Rabelais' *Gargantua* (1534): an unidentified speaker shouts it out when someone else cries for a page to refill his cup with wine. By making a joke of the idea, Rabelais indicates that the Latin phrase was already well known, and already meant what we mean by it today: nature tends to fill up empty space with stuff.

An English version appears slightly later, in 1550, which is also the first occurrence of the word "vacuum" in our language. Thomas Cranmer, Archbishop of Canterbury, wrote that "Natural reason abhoreth *vacuum*, that is to say, that there should be any empty place, wherein no substance should be." Cranmer treats "vacuum" as a Latin term; it wasn't fully welcomed as an English word in its own right until about 1607.

Nothing Comes from Nothing

We will now consider imperceptible things. In the first place, nothing is born of nothing; otherwise, everything would be born of everything, without any need for seeds. And if that which disappears from view perished into non-being, all things would have died, since that into which they dissolved would not be. Thus, everything has always been as it is now, and will always be thus.

Epicurus, *Letter to Herodotus*, sections 38–39

Others before, and others since, Epicurus [*see* EPICUREAN] recognized the fundamental physical principle modern science calls the Law of the Conservation of Energy. The notion seems to have first been put forth in the sixth century B.C., for example by Xenophanes, who, besides being the first authentic theologian and anticipating monotheism, is reported to have said that "what comes to be must come from what already is."

Later, Empedocles (fifth century B.C.) stated in no uncertain terms that "They are fools, incapable of deep thoughts, who firmly believe that what does not exist can come into being, or that what exists can entirely perish and be destroyed"; in other words, "it is inconceivable that something could come to be from what does not at all exist."

Xenophanes did not stop at physics; he used the idea that nothing comes from nothing to prove that the gods, or the one God, cannot have been created. God must have always existed, along with the basic matter of nature, for if not, where did created things come from? The same argument would be restated by medieval Christian thinkers, who supposed they were onto something new. But nothing comes from nothing.

The Seven Sages of Greece

Many today and in earlier ages have noted that the true Spartan type of character has the love of philosophy even stronger than the love of gymnastics. . . . Among such men were Thales of Miletus, Pittacus of Mytilene, Bias of Priene, our own Solon, Cleobulus of Lindus, and Myson of Chen, and seventh in the catalogue of wise men was a Spartan, Chilon. All these were lovers and emulators and disciples of Spartan culture, and anyone may perceive that their wisdom was of this character, consisting of short, memorable sentences uttered by each. And they met together and dedicated in the temple of Apollo at Delphi, as the first fruits of their wisdom, the far-famed inscriptions, which are in all men's mouths, "Know thyself" and "Nothing too much."

Plato, *Protagoras*

By way of praising the laconic style of his predecessors [*see* LACONIC], Socrates incidentally provides us with the earliest surviving list of the so-called Seven Sages of Greece, famous wise men of the sixth century B.C. Later authorities juggle the names somewhat, substituting Periander or Anacharsis for Myson. That's all Greek to me, and to you too I suppose; the major figures among the seven—Thales, Solon, and Chilon— are in any case agreed upon by all.

Socrates refers to these men as philosophers, but they probably never thought of themselves as such; they were too busy with politics. Solon, for example, had his hands full reforming the Athenian constitution [*see* DRACONIAN], while Chilon was an ephor or magistrate at Sparta, where he attempted to reinforce the city's traditional discipline [*see* SPEAK WELL OF THE DEAD]. Nonetheless, there is a wide body of pithy, quasi-philosophical sayings attributed to the group—much of it standard stuff by now, but there are a few outstanding lines [*see* KNOW THYSELF *and* NOTHING IN EXCESS].

Socrates obliquely refers to the most interesting story about the Seven Sages. According to legend, as later reported by

Diogenes Laertius, some Ionian youths bought a catch of fish from Milesian fishermen, and found among the take a golden tripod. A dispute arose as to who should rightfully take possession of the windfall, and the question was referred to the Oracle at Delphi. Apollo replied with these verses: "Who shall possess the tripod? . . . 'Whosoever is most wise.'" The tripod was first presented to Thales, who refused the honor; the same scenario was repeated with each of the other six sages. When the tripod came into Solon's hands, he declared that it was Apollo himself that was most wise, and sent it back to Delphi. In Plato's version of the story, all seven sages later joined together at Delphi to dedicate their wise sayings to the god.

In addition to "know thyself" and "nothing in excess," sayings attributed to the sages include: "master anger," "look to the end of life," "avoid responsibility for others' debts," and the characteristically Greek "most men are bad."

Skepticism

Many names of philosophical schools have become almost completely detached from meaning; today's "stoic" has little relation to a painted portico [*see* p. 78], nor does the "cynic" spend time in a Greek gymnasium, barking [*see* p. 55]. But "skepticism" actually describes an enduring condition rather than a forgotten place or long-dead philosopher: the Greek *skeptikoi* were "the inquirers," or "the hesitants." But while today's skeptic is certainly hesitant, we must remember that the Greeks were true professionals.

Pyrrhon of Elis (ca. 365–275 B.C.), the founding skeptic, did not become famous just for looking askance at optimistic statements. Rather, he believed that experience presents to the mind so many contradictions that true knowledge about anything is impossible. If we only have experience to go by, then we are forced to give up on the idea of certain truth. Later, skepticism came to refer to a toned-down version of Pyrrhon's philosophy, which still held in doubt the power of naked reason, but admitted that working knowledge could be drawn from experience.

The modern sense of "skepticism" began developing in the seventeenth century, when the word was gradually limited to doubt about the claims of a particular field of knowledge—theology, for example. "First bring in skepticism in doctrine and looseness of life," wrote Thomas Edwards in 1646, "and afterwards all atheism." Fear of this sort of skepticism is hardly extinct, but today's skeptic is less likely to be so systematically doubtful. Skepticism has become a kind of free-floating wariness toward particular claims, rather than thorough doubt about the possibility of true knowledge.

Sophism

Sneering at sophism is one of mankind's oldest hobbies—over twenty-four centuries old, to be precise. Yet the word "sophism" itself derives from the Greek *sophos*, "wise"; a "sophist" is thus a "wise man" (just as "*philo-sophia*" is "love of wisdom"). Today's sophist dresses lies in a suit of rationality; the original sophists were the revered and very wise Seven Sages of Greece [*see* p. 72]. But by the mid-fifth century B.C., "sophist" was the name given to a professional wise man who sold his "wisdom." As time went on, the sophists concentrated less on wisdom and more on rhetoric, the art of making a convincing case for any cause, good or bad. The sophists, that is, became instructors in propaganda.

That, in any case, is the argument of Socrates in Plato's dialogues *Theaetetus*, *Protagoras*, and *Sophist*. The most famous of the early sophists, Protagoras, comes in for especially harsh criticism. Protagoras had advanced the notion that "man is the measure of all things" [*see* p. 89]—in other words, that whether something is true or false, good or evil, depends on how we perceive it. The wise man, accordingly, argues for what is expedient, rather than wasting his time searching out absolute good or absolute truth. In the hands of Protagoras's more extreme successors, sophism started to look pretty irresponsible.

By the fourteenth century in England, "sophism" and "sophistry" had become terms of opprobrium, referring to deliberately false reasoning, especially impious false reasoning. In 1532, Sir Thomas More accused the early Protestants of turning "earnest Godly sentence [wisdom]" into "frivolous cavillations and sophisms." These sophists, he sneered, could with a foolish argument prove "that two eggs were three."

Despite, or perhaps because of, its negative connotations, the word "sophister," another term for sophistical arguers, became by the 1570s the common term for a student in his second year at Cambridge University. Later, second-year students at Oxford, Harvard, and Dartmouth were also bestowed with the epithet "sophister." But by the late seventeenth century at Cambridge, and by the early eighteenth century at American colleges, "sophister" was replaced by "sophomore." Though the *Oxford English Dictionary* derives "sophomore" from "sophism" plus "-or," others have more persuasively argued that the "-more" of "sophomore" derives from the Greek *moros*, "foolish." Thus a sophomore is a "wise fool" or, to stick closer to the Greek, a "wise moron."

Speak Well of the Dead

Here are some of Chilon's precepts: "Hold your tongue, above all at a banquet; do not malign your neighbor if you don't want to hear distressing words in return; threaten no one, because that's a woman's behavior; be more attentive to your friends when they are unhappy than when they are happy; marry modestly; speak no evil of the dead; honor old age; keep a watch on yourself . . . ."

Diogenes Laertius, Lives of Eminent Philosophers, Book 1, chapter 3

According to the Spartan magistrate and philosopher Chilon (sixth century B.C.), man's excellence lies in using reason to divine the future. Not a whole lot more is known about him except that he was strict; we are left with only a few aphorisms from the man Herodotus claimed was the wisest of the Seven Sages of Greece [see p. 72].

Even from the brief sample I've excerpted out of Diogenes' biography, you'll notice that Chilon sticks closely to traditional social values. The most famous piece of advice from this list is "speak no evil of the dead." Chilon's precept became a catch-phrase in Greece and later in Rome, and thereafter passed into Renaissance proverb books. Richard Taverner supplied the first English translation in 1540: "Rail not upon him that is dead."

In 1669 William Penn—the Quaker leader who later founded the great state of Pennsylvania—transformed Chilon's negative advice into its more familiar positive version: "Chilon . . . would say . . . 'Speak well of the dead.'"

Stoic

The word "stoic," by which we mean "indifferent to pleasure and pain," actually derives from the *Stoa Poikile* in Athens, which was a portico (*stoa*) painted (*poikile*) with scenes of the destruction of Troy [*see* THE TROJAN WAR]. Here, late in the fourth century B.C., the philosopher Zeno of Citium—not to be confused with Zeno of Elea [*see* p. 81]—began teaching the doctrines later called "stoic." According to Zeno, God infuses and animates the world, and thus the virtuous life is most in accord with natural law. Since nature itself is divine, it is perfect, and so it's no use trying to impose your desires on it. Stoicism thus became a philosophy of apathy, the indifference to passions and cares. Wisdom is knowing to take things as they come.

The Romans were especially taken by these teachings, which agreed with their notions of self-sacrifice. The emperor Marcus Aurelius himself (second century A.D.) was one of the greatest Stoic authors, if one of the last. Renaissance England's reception of Zeno's teachings, however, was less enthusiastic. Even while they resurrected the doctrine, the authors of the day were in fact rather cool to the idea of Stoic indifference, usually portraying it as impossible to attain and thus a vanity. Francis Bacon, in his essay "On Anger" (1625), pronounces that "To seek to extinguish anger utterly, is but a bravery [boast] of the Stoics." The poet Alexander Pope disdained Stoicism as bloodlessness: "In lazy Apathy let Stoics boast/ Their virtue fixed; 'tis fix'd as in a frost." (*An Essay on Man*, 1733). But there has always been a hint of admiration buried in the scorn; and today, though we decry apathy, we can't help but admire the stoic virtue of endurance.

The Transmigration of Souls

When the soul has been violently expelled and thrown to earth, it wanders through the airs like some phantom. Hermes is the steward of souls . . . and he guides them from their bodies by land and by sea, and conducts pure souls toward the highest of heavens, and forbids impure souls from going with the others, or from grouping together, but on the contrary brings them to the Furies to be bound by indestructible bonds. All the air is filled with souls called *daimones;* it is they who bring dreams to men, and signs of sickness and health, and not only to men, but also to beasts.

Diogenes Laertius, *Lives of Eminent Philosophers,* Book 8, chapter 1

Those of us who have suffered through geometry class will best remember Pythagoras (sixth century B.C.) for his equation relating the sides of a right triangle; but in former times he was famous more for his metaphysical doctrines than for his mathematical ones. Diogenes Laertius tells part of the story here, a part earlier referred to by Plato: after death, according to Pythagoras, the soul wanders the earth until it is brought by the god Hermes into some sort of heaven for its final rest, or is sent to the Furies (rather unfriendly goddesses) to be bound up in chains.

But this is not the end of the story for those impure souls who don't make Hermes' cut. First, they are put through a painful rite of purification, and then each is sent back to earth as either a human being or an animal. Thus they're given one more chance to behave themselves, and if they are pure enough the next time they die, they'll be allowed to join the company of the elect in forming the universal soul of which all individual souls are mere fragments. (Note: according to Pythagoras, eating meat or beans is a good way to accrue impurities, so it should be avoided. The animal you eat may be your grandfather.) This cycling through bodies has become known as "the transmigration of souls," or *metempsychosis* in Greek.

This idea, while it became directly associated with Pythagoras, did not originate with him, but was adopted from earlier religious doctrine called "Orphism." Herodotus, in his *Histories* (Book 2), traces the belief to the Egyptians, but it also appears independently in the Indian Upanishads (ca. 900 B.C.) and in Jewish Cabbalism. Once you allow for the immortality of the soul, it's a short step to assuming its preexistence, though that premise has been excised from Western religious thought.

Zeno's Paradox

Zeno of Elea (fifth century B.C.), who preceded his stoic namesake by about 150 years [*see* p. 78], specialized in paradoxes—indeed, paradox was his philosophy. So while there is no one "Zeno's paradox," the most famous of them, a paradox of motion, has taken that name.

As Zeno pointed out, if you wish to travel from one point to another, first you must travel half the distance. To travel the rest of the way, first you must travel half of the way left, in other words, another quarter of the way. To travel the rest of the way, you must travel half of the way left, in other words, another eighth of the way; and so on, ad infinitum. In other words, no matter how close you get to the second point, you still have to travel half the distance left, and you will find yourself in this situation forever. Therefore, Zeno triumphantly concluded, motion is impossible, since you can never get where you're going, even if it's an inch away.

Another, and perhaps more familiar, version of the paradox involves a race between Achilles and a tortoise, similar in

outcome to Aesop's race of the tortoise and the hare, but with a different moral. If Achilles, feeling uncharacteristically generous, gives the tortoise a head-start, he can never win. Let us assume that Achilles begins running at 1:00. To catch up, he must first reach the place where the tortoise was at 1:00, but that may take ten minutes. But in that ten minutes, the tortoise has of course kept going, so Achilles, to catch up, must now reach the point where the tortoise was at 1:10. This will take some time, say five minutes. But in that five minutes, the tortoise has lumbered farther along toward the finish line, and now Achilles must race to where the tortoise was at 1:15. And so on. Therefore, Zeno triumphantly concluded, the common sense that would predict Achilles' victory is contradicted by the laws of motion; therefore, our ideas of motion are wrong.

Now, we can be pretty sure that Zeno got around, and that he used motion to do it. He may have even walked past a few tortoises in his time. His aim in propounding this paradox was ultimately to support the doctrines of his mentor Parmenides, who had very abstract notions of motion, being, not being, and time. Zeno was gifted with both wit and a concrete imagination, which makes him a formidable opponent of Socrates in Plato's dialogue *Parmenides*.

Plato

(ca. 428–348 B.C.)

Like many a young Athenian aristocrat of the late fifth century B.C., Plato fell under the influence of a physically unattractive gadfly named Socrates (469–399 B.C.), who also happened to be an extraordinarily powerful and seductive thinker. Virtually everything we know about Socrates is derived from the voluminous writings of Plato, who recorded his master's philosophy in a series of twenty-five dialogues, plus a reconstruction of Socrates' defense before the Athenian jury that would condemn him to death.

In 399 B.C., Socrates was hauled into court on charges of heresy and of corrupting the youth of Athens. The suit seems to have been motivated by both pique and politics, since Socrates took few pains to conceal his contempt for public opinion and for Athens' random variety of democracy. His circle also included a number of so-called "enemies to the state," haughty and independent aristocrats like Alcibiades [see PLATONIC LOVE], as well as the less openly rebellious Plato. Socrates was condemned, but Plato wasn't there to see it—he was feeling a little ill that day.

How closely Plato's Socrates resembles the real man is difficult to say, since the development of Plato's own thought finds expression in Socrates' increasingly sophisticated teachings in the dialogues. But there can be no doubt that Socrates did indeed employ the "Socratic method," whereby the master lectures his students by asking them leading questions and exploring the consequences of their answers. And Plato's representation of Socrates' wit and self-deprecating irony (he once said that "all I know is that I know nothing") is certainly true to the man.

As for philosophical ideas, Plato may base them on Socrates' teachings, but he advances them to a new degree. Plato's most important idea concerns Ideas (or Ideals) themselves, which are eternal, perfect, and ultimately more real than ordinary things or opinions [*see* PLATO'S CAVE]. And Plato himself is certainly the creator of the ideal state he has Socrates describe in *Republic*—a state ruled by a philosopher king [*see* p. 91].

Plato did more than theorize about such a republic; he somewhat foolishly tried to put it into action. His guinea pig was the tyrant Dionysius II of Syracuse, son of the whimsically brutal Dionysius I [*see* A SWORD OF DAMOCLES]. With the help of the tyrant's relative Dion, Plato tried to mold the young ruler into a philosopher king, but utterly failed. Dionysius turned out to be so bad, in fact, that Dion was compelled to topple him as the frustrated and distressed Plato watched from the sidelines. When Dion himself turned into a rather unphilosophical tyrant, he was assassinated by a certain Callippus, who happened to be one of Plato's students. Small wonder that in what is apparently his last dialogue, *Laws*, Plato abandons much of *Republic*'s idealism and strenuously insists on the rule of law.

The Groves of Academe

It happened that I was nurtured at Rome, and was taught
How much the wrath of Achilles had injured the Greeks.
Good Athens contributed a bit more to my skill,
So that I wished to distinguish virtue from vice
And to seek the truth among the groves of Academe.

Horace, *Epistles*, Book 2, epistle 2, lines 41–45

The poet Horace tells us how, as a philosophically inclined youth, he joyfully roamed through "the groves of Academe." Those who have had close brushes with today's institutions of higher learning may find Horace's eulogy curious, but he isn't talking about any old academy.

In ancient times, "The Academy" or "Academe" referred principally to Plato's philosophical school, located in an olive grove just outside Athens. This grove was dedicated to the legendary hero Academicus, who was supposed to have once come to the aid of Zeus's daughter Helen (the one who inspired the Trojan War). Amidst the olive trees in "the shady walks of the divine Academus," as the Greek dramatist Eupolis (fifth century B.C.) referred to them, was a gymnasium, and here Plato set up shop in the early fourth century. The place soon became a magnet for aspiring intellectuals, including Aristotle.

Although Plato's own philosophy was idealistic, his successors turned the Academy into a breeding ground of skepticism [*see* p. 74]. So while it is understandable that Horace would seek out the ancient groves to bask in a little philosophical glamor, he chose a strange place to go seeking the truth.

A Cup of Hemlock

A servant went out and, having been absent for some time, returned with the jailer carrying the cup of poison. Socrates said: "You, my good friend, who are experienced in these matters, must direct me on how to proceed." The man answered: "You have only to walk about until your legs are heavy, and then to lie down, and the poison will act."

Plato, *Phaedo*

Socrates, convicted of heresy and of corrupting Athens' youth, has been condemned to die [*see* THE UNEXAMINED LIFE IS NOT WORTH LIVING]. As per the usual method of capital punishment, Socrates is required to drink a cup of poison—which he does readily, since he's convinced the afterlife will be quite a bit more pleasant than life in Athens [*see* A SWAN SONG]. That the poison was hemlock, Plato himself does not say in his account of Socrates' last days. The Latin philosopher and historian Pliny the Elder, however, does report in his *Natural History* that Athenian law forced malefactors "to drink that odious potion of hemlock."

The hemlock plant—or *Conium maculatum*—was not referred to in English writing as poisonous until about the sixteenth century; before that, it was regarded as, at worst, a weed and, at best, a medicinal herb. But, especially in latter times, the popular legend of Socrates' death has made the word "hemlock" synonymous with the poisonous extract rather than the plant itself. Its anesthetic effects are famously described by the poet Keats in his *Ode to a Nightingale*: "A drowsy numbness pains/ My sense, as though of hemlock I had drunk."

Gyges' Ring

According to the tradition, Gyges was a shepherd in the service of the king of Lydia; there was a great storm, and an earthquake made an opening in the earth at the place where he was feeding his flock. Amazed at the sight, he descended into the opening, where, among other marvels, he beheld a hollow brazen horse with doors. Gyges stooped down and, looking in, saw a dead body of stature, which appeared to him more than human, and which had nothing on but a gold ring. He took this ring from the finger of the corpse and reascended.

Plato, *Republic*, Book 2

Socrates uses the shepherd Gyges to exemplify that, as the Catholic historian Lord Acton would say in 1887, "Power tends to corrupt and absolute power corrupts absolutely." It turns out that the ring Gyges finds lets him become invisible at will. What does Gyges do with this power? He goes to court, seduces the queen, conspires to kill the king, and takes over the kingdom of Lydia (now in western Turkey). Gyges, according to Socrates, merely behaves as any man would if given the same power, whether he had been thought just or unjust before. Socrates concludes that men are just only when they must be, and are unjust whenever they safely can.

Herodotus also tells the story of Gyges in his *Histories* (Book 1), but omits mention of the ring. Nonetheless, the legend—referred to in English by 1586—has lent us a metaphor for an interloper's power to sneak around undetected. Gyges' ring is a distant relative of "the cap of Hades" or "helmet of Pluto," mentioned in Homer's *Iliad* (Book 5), which Athena borrows so that she might, by virtue of its powers of invisibility, evade the war god Ares.

To Make the Worse Appear
the Better Cause

Well, what do the slanderers say? Since they shall be my prosecutors, let me sum up their words as in an affidavit: "Socrates is an evil-doer, and a curious person, who searches into things under the earth and in the heaven, and he makes the worse appear the better cause; and he teaches the aforesaid doctrines to others." Such is the accusation.

Plato, *Apology (Socrates' Defense)*

Socrates stands accused as a menace to the Athenian state, a charge that will result in his being condemned to death [*see* THE UNEXAMINED LIFE IS NOT WORTH LIVING *and* A CUP OF HEMLOCK]. Plato's *Apology* records Socrates' eloquent, if futile, refutation of the charges, which he characterizes as the ignorant slanders of malicious critics. One baseless charge is that Socrates "makes the worse appear the better cause."

To make the worse appear the better cause is to deliberately promote an evil in the guise of a seeming good. This charge must be particularly galling to the philosopher, who in several of Plato's dialogues levels the same accusation at a group known as the Sophists [*see* p. 75]. Though the original Sophists had claimed to teach wisdom, Socrates' contemporaries trained their customers in the amoral arts of rhetorical argumentation, whose object is to win an audience over to a position whether or not that position is healthy, good for the state, or true. Contemporary readers will notice a distinct similarity between the Greeks' "sophism" and what we call the practice of the law.

Man Is the Measure of All Things

SOCRATES: Can I ever fail of knowing that which I perceive?

THEAETETUS: You cannot.

SOCRATES: Then you were quite right in affirming that knowledge is only perception; and the meaning turns out to be the same, whether with Homer and Heraclitus, and all that company, you say that all is motion and flux, or with the great sage Protagoras, that man is the measure of all things; or with Theaetetus, that, granting these premises, perception is knowledge.

Plato, *Theaetetus*

If you're familiar at all with Socrates' technique, you will already have guessed that he's setting up Theaetetus for a fall. The idea that "man is the measure of all things" strikes Socrates as vain as well as false; but rather than just saying so outright he gently steers his young interlocutor by way of the "Socratic method" so that Theaetetus will come to really understand why it is false. By the end, neither of them has determined the truth, but at least they agree that Protagoras was wrong.

Protagoras (ca. 480–411 B.C.) was one the first and greatest Sophists [*see* p. 75], who believed that wisdom could be taught (for a price)—a radical idea at the time. The founding principle of Protagoras's philosophy is that "man is the measure of all things"; in other words, things exist by virtue of how we perceive them. The object world is measured against man, and there is nothing outside man that determines being or truth. This rather abstract idea, which is anathema to Socrates' notion of Ideals [*see* PLATO'S CAVE] has surprisingly become a popular catch-phrase. But what we seem to mean by it today is that "our needs and desires determine what counts in this world."

Might Makes Right

"Listen, then," Thrasymachus said; "I proclaim that justice is nothing else than the interest of the stronger."

Plato, *Republic*, Book 1

That might makes right had already been demonstrated by Aesop's lion [*see* THE LION'S SHARE] and lamented by Hesiod in his *Works and Days*. But the most extensive discussion of this troubling idea is presented by Plato in the *Republic*, in which Socrates works up quite a knot of syllogisms to disprove Thrasymachus's claim that power is justice, strength is law. Socrates' main contention is that the exercise of naked power leads to injuries, and the injured man cannot be said to have been justly served. But right cannot produce wrong, so therefore might cannot in itself make right. Furthermore, injustice tends to the destruction of the state; this view is paraphrased in an early English song of the fourteenth century, in the earliest surviving instance of the phrase: "For [if] might is right, the land is lawless."

The words "might makes right" themselves probably derive from the first-century poet Lucan's expression, *Mensura iuris vis est*—"Might is the measure of right." Lucan conjured the phrase from bitter experience, having developed a rivalry with his patron, the emperor Nero. As Tacitus describes the situation, "Nero, who vainly supposed himself Lucan's peer as a poet, cut down Lucan's reputation and ordered him to avoid publicity." Such indignities drove Lucan into a conspiracy which, when discovered, cost him his life.

A Philosopher King

I said: "Until philosophers are kings, or the kings and princes of this world have the spirit and power of philosophy, and political greatness and wisdom meet in one, and those commoner natures who pursue either to the exclusion of the other are compelled to stand aside, cities will never have rest from their evils—no, nor the human race, as I believe—and then only will this our State have a possibility of life and behold the light of day."

Plato, *Republic*, Book 5

The idea of a "philosopher king," first proposed by Socrates in Plato's *Republic*, is apt to strike today's reader as quite humorous. Few modern examples present themselves. Anyway, people would rather their king (or their president, or their congressman, or their M.P. for that matter) be efficient than wise. As Louis MacNeice put it in his *Autumn Journal*, "Good-bye now, Plato and Hegel,/ The shop is closing down;/ They don't want any philosopher-kings in England,/ There ain't no universals in this man's town."

What Socrates means by "philosopher" is someone who loves and pursues the Good by loving and pursuing wisdom. Only knowledge enables you to distinguish truth from falsehood and mere opinion; and only love of wisdom, which is spiritual, frees you from the corruptions that worldly desires breed. The philosopher, furthermore, is not a political animal [*see* p. 101]: shunning the ignorant opinions of the multitude, he is not ruled by their desires (in other words, he couldn't care less about public opinion polls). By consorting with the Good, or divine perfection, only the philosopher is capable of true justice.

Socrates freely admits that no existing state is quite ready for a philosopher king; that's why he has to invent a new state in this dialogue, and he comes up with one of the first utopias in literature.

Platonic Love

"When it seemed to me that he was smitten, and that my arrows had wounded him, I got up, and throwing my coat about him crept under his threadbare cloak, as it was winter, and there I lay during the whole night having this wonderful monster in my arms. You will not deny it, Socrates. And yet, notwithstanding all, he was so superior to my solicitations, so contemptuous and derisive and disdainful of my beauty . . . that in the morning when I awoke (let all the gods and goddesses be my witness) I arose as from the couch of a father or an elder brother."

Plato, *Symposium*

Today we gather for symposia on such momentous issues as "Luxembourg's Banking Laws in a Unified European Market." But to the Greeks a symposium was primarily a drinking party, which happened to inspire witty conversation. (Not until the nineteenth century did "symposium" assume its current, alcohol-free meaning.) At the symposium Plato depicts in this dialogue, the participants—among them Socrates, the comic dramatist Aristophanes, and the Athenian general Alcibiades—do plenty of drinking, by virtue of which their talk turns to the nature of love.

It was not unusual at this time in Greece for boys and young men to become romantically attached to an older man, who was known as the "lover." In the higher social strata, this custom was tacitly approved, and justified as affording more stable and beneficial relationships than did attachments to women—who were considered of inferior spiritual quality. But where the lover ordinarily had to woo his beloved, Alcibiades describes the frustrating experience of having to woo his lover Socrates. And as we learn here, he didn't have much luck. The sort of love Socrates gives to Alcibiades, in which the sexual motive is absent, is what we now call "Platonic love," after this dialogue.

In the Platonic view of things, true love strives after the Idea of Beauty, which is synonymous with divinity. To reach this ideal, the lover must wean himself of fleshly desires. The lover will at first be attracted to his beloved's physical beauty; but ideally he will then begin to recognize in the beloved a spiritual beauty, which is purer and therefore better than mere physical beauty. Once the lover achieves this much, he may then come to realize that spiritual beauty flows from a higher source—the Idea of Beauty. Socrates himself aims for union with the Idea of Beauty, which he equates with true knowledge; but what we call "Platonic love" is only the intermediate stage of attraction to a particular beloved's spiritual beauty. (Try remembering that the next time a love interest eagerly suggests you become "really good friends.")

The phrase "Platonic love" itself derives from *amor platonicus*, coined by the fifteenth-century Italian philosopher Marsilio Ficino. Given the sexual predilections of Greek men, he meant an inclination to pederasty rather than absence of sexual desire. English use of the term, however, has since its introduction in the seventeenth century principally meant the latter. As John Norris wrote in 1678, "Platonic Love is the love of Beauty abstracted from all sensual Applications, and desire of Corporal Contact."

The idea is nice but the practice more troublesome. Those of us less high-minded than Socrates are likely to agree with the sentiments of Samuel Richardson's Mr. B., who decides "that Platonic love is Platonic nonsense: 'tis but the fly buzzing about the blaze, till its wings are scorched" (*Pamela*, 1740). As Sir Philip Sidney wrote in the sixteenth century, "So while thy beauty draws the heart to love,/ As fast thy Virtue bends that love to good:/ But ah, Desire still cries, give me some food" (*Astrophil and Stella*).

Plato's Cave

"And now," I said, "let me show in a figure how far our nature is enlightened or unenlightened: Behold! human beings living in an underground den, which has a mouth open towards the light and reaching all along the den; here they have been from their childhood, and have their legs and necks chained so that they cannot move, and can only see before them, being prevented by the chains from turning round their heads. Above and behind them a fire is blazing at a distance, and between the fire and the prisoners there is a raised way; and you will see, if you look, a low wall built along the way, like the screen which marionette players have in front of them, over which they show the puppets. . . . [They are like ourselves,] and they see only their own shadows, or the shadows of one another, which the fire throws on the opposite wall of the cave."

Plato, *Republic*, Book 7

Socrates' elaborate metaphor of the underground cave with its shadows on the wall is the most famous explanation of his notion of ideal forms. In Plato's scheme, the objects in our world are mere imitations (or "shadows") of unchanging, eternal forms. And we are like prisoners in a dark cave, our intellects chained, mistaking the shadows of being for being itself. The desk I'm sitting at now, for example, is merely the imitation of an ideal desk, which can never change, which exists in eternity, and on which I can never spill coffee. This ideal desk is not a phantasm; it is in fact more "real" than the desk itself, because it is more universal—it inspires all desk-makers to produce their imperfect, coffee-stainable imitations. Yet we commonly mistake these imitations for "real" desks, because from birth we've had our sights trained only on the world of imitations, unable to rise above them and enter the world of Ideas.

Just so, the prisoners in Plato's cave, chained in place, have only ever seen passing shadows on the wall, which they naturally mistake for the bodies that cast those shadows. If they were set free and allowed to turn toward the light at the mouth of the cave, at first the sight would be painful and disorienting, but soon their eyes would adapt and they could begin to perceive and recognize the persons and objects around them. Even then, they would still insist on the "reality" or "superior truth" of the shadows; but if their liberators dragged them out into the full sunlight, they would eventually come around to the right view of things and pity their former state.

As Socrates explains, we too may be set free, by philosophy. Philosophy drags us out of the gloom of our cave of ignorance and confronts us with the truth of being. At last we perceive the master idea, the Being of beings: "in the world of knowledge the idea of the good appears last of all, and is seen only with effort; and, when seen, is also inferred to be the universal author of all things beautiful and right, parent of light and the lord of light in this visible world."

A Swan Song

Will you not, Simmias, allow that I have as much of the spirit of prophecy as do the swans? For they, when they perceive that they must die, having sung all their life long, do then sing more, and more sweetly, than ever, rejoicing in the thought that they are about to go away to Apollo, whose ministers they are. But men, because they fear death, slanderously accuse the swans of singing laments at the last.

Plato, Phaedo

You'd think impending death would sober the philosopher Socrates [*see* A CUP OF HEMLOCK], but instead he prepares to sing his "swan song." In the company of his friends and pupils, the condemned man jovially explains why he welcomes death. According to the natural history of the time, swans were thought to belt out their best song just before dying; and according to Socrates, this is a joyful song anticipating a reunion with their patron god Apollo. Socrates too is dedicated to Apollo, god of philosophy as well as of light, prophecy, and music. "I am no worse endowed with prophetic powers by my master than they are," he says, "and no more disconsolate at leaving this life."

Unfortunately, however, swans may honk, but you wouldn't call that singing—*pace* Aeschylus, Aristotle, Cicero, Chaucer, Shakespeare, and the host of other geniuses who repeated the tale. (Shakespeare may be the prime beneficiary of the swan legend, since the idea that Apollo sent the souls of dead poets into the bodies of swans is the basis for the Bard's epithet "the Swan of Avon," coined by Ben Jonson.) Chaucer was the first English writer to refer to the legend, but Thomas Carlyle, adapting a German phrase, was the first to use "swan song" itself, in *Sartor Resartus* (1831).

The Unexamined Life
Is Not Worth Living

Someone will say: "Socrates, if you hold your tongue, you may go to a foreign city, and no one will interfere with you." Now I have great difficulty in making you understand my answer to this. For if I tell you that to do as you say would be a disobedience to the god, and therefore that I cannot hold my tongue, you will not believe that I am serious. And if I say again that the greatest good of man is daily to converse about virtue, and all those subjects concerning which you hear me examining myself and others, and that the unexamined life is not worth living, you are still less likely to believe me.

Plato, *Apology (Socrates' Defense)*

In the Athenian judicial system, the accused had to defend himself unaided before the jury. Typical defenses consisted of abject flattery of the jurors and pathetic self-abasement; Socrates, however, up on charges of heresy and of corrupting Athens' youth, takes a more confrontational approach, which will of course seal his doom. In this passage, he rejects his accusers' generous offer of exile, pointing out that wherever he should go he would be incapable of minding his own business—that is, incapable of staying out of the trouble that's landed him in court. If his crime is, as it seems, questioning the received wisdom of the state, he chooses to die: "the unexamined life is not worth living."

For Socrates, the issue is literally a matter of life and death. We use the phrase today somewhat differently—less seriously, more personally, and hardly in a political sense. "The unexamined life is not worth living" is usually a defense of more harmless, and more self-indulgent, sorts of philosophical inquiry.

ARISTOTLE

(384–322 B.C.)

By the time he founded the Peripatetic school of philosophy in 335 B.C. [*see* p. 103], Aristotle had already built up a solid résumé. One of Plato's star students, Aristotle left the Academy [*see* p. 85] upon his teacher's death to join a rival Platonic school, but then retired to Lesbos [*see* LESBIAN] to pursue zoological interests inherited from his father. His studies were soon interrupted, however, when in 343 he was summoned by King Philip of Macedonia to tutor the young prince Alexander—later Alexander the Great.

Aristotle's tutoring forced him to think a little harder about politics and literature (he inspired in Alexander a lifelong love of Homer, and especially of the hero Achilles). As a result, Aristotle would later write the basic classical texts on those "sciences"—the *Politics* and the *Poetics*. But he wrote on just about everything else, too, turning out dozens of manuscripts on topics such as the soul, memory, ethics, physics, sleep, dreams, respiration, zoology, animal reproduction, and metaphysics.

Aristotle's work is characterized by its mania for classification and definition, which formed the basis of the logically oriented scientific methods practiced in the West until the late seventeenth century. Indeed, Aristotle, known as "The Philosopher," was accepted as the ultimate authority in almost every field of philosophy and science until the late Renaissance period.

Traditionally depicted as bald, scrawny, and lisping, Aristotle lived to the age of sixty-three, when he died of an intestinal disease.

Art Imitates Nature

"Nature" may signify either "material" or "form." . . . In reading the ancients one might well suppose that the physicist's only concern was with the material. . . . But if art imitates nature, and if in the arts and crafts it pertains to the same branch of knowledge to study the form and, up to a point, the material . . . it seems to follow that physics must take cognizance both of the formal and of the material aspect of nature.

Aristotle, *Physics*, Book 2, chapter 2

Aristotle's discussion of physical science may seem so abstract as to be pointless, but it will appear a model of clarity if you've tried delving into the subtleties of recent cosmological debates. Indeed, his picture of the universe is relatively simple, since it involves only two basic elements: matter and form.

According to Aristotle, nothing in nature is purely matter or purely form. So he disagrees with the contention that physicists should be concerned only with matter. If artificial objects are of the same kind as natural ones—that is, if "art imitates nature"— then the physicist's knowledge of nature must be of the same kind as the artist's knowledge of his materials. Just as a builder must know both the form and the matter of the house he builds—its structure as well as its bricks and beams—the physicist must know both the form and the matter of nature.

The somehow compelling commonplace that "art imitates nature" has been simplified over the years. Aristotle doesn't mean that works of art merely copy the forms of natural objects, but that the artistic process imitates the natural process of creation. Where Plato insisted that works of art are only flawed imitations of more perfect originals, Aristotle elevates artificial objects to the level of natural objects.

A Lyceum

If you have a lyceum in the neighborhood, it's most likely a small lecture hall or library, a monument to the community's respect for knowledge. But the first Lyceum was, like Plato's Academy [*see* p. 85], a gymnasium, situated in a grove outside Athens and named for the god Apollo, one of whose epithets was "Lykeius" (compounded from the Greek words for "wolf-slayer" and "god of light").

As the Academy was to Plato, the Lyceum was to Aristotle, Plato's star pupil. After leaving the Academy and serving as tutor to Prince Alexander of Macedonia, Aristotle returned to Athens to start his own school at the Lyceum. While there, he developed a philosophy based on Plato's but much less idealistic. His teachings, later called "peripatetic" [*see* p. 103], dealt primarily with natural philosophy and common experience, rather than with transcendental truths, as had Plato's.

In France, a *lycée* is simply a high school; English and American lyceums are specialized products of the nineteenth century. In England, lyceums served as forums for literary lectures, while the Americans characteristically bent their purpose to popular improvement. Harriet Martineau in 1837 described the project of a lyceum as the "instruction of working men." Expectations were high, as W. R. Williams noted in 1854: "Men have expected . . . the Lyceum and the Lecture to close the dram-shop"—that is, to shut down the local bar. The outcome of this contest should have been obvious; today lyceums are dedicated to less idealistic projects. How Aristotelian.

Man Is a Political Animal

When several villages are united in a single complete community, large enough to be nearly or quite self-sufficing, the state comes into existence, originating in the bare needs of life, and continuing in existence for the sake of a good life. And therefore, if the earlier forms of society are natural, so is the state, for it is the end of them, and the nature of a thing is its end. ... Hence it is evident that the state is a creation of nature, and that man is by nature a political animal. And he who by nature and not by mere accident is without a state, is either a bad man or above humanity.

Aristotle, *Politics*, Book 1, chapter 2

Aristotle's *Politics*, a work of anthropology as much as of political science, is based on the famous idea that "man is by nature a political animal." He doesn't mean that we naturally crave to attend party conventions, but rather that we naturally tend to organize and ultimately to associate politically under the auspices of a state.

The building block of the state is the patriarchal household, which serves the family's basic needs and provides protection. Households naturally band together into villages, which are capable of satisfying a broader range of needs and of achieving a greater good. Finally, villages naturally tend to unite themselves "in a single complete community" which is relatively self-sufficient. As the ultimate expression of human nature, the state is Aristotle's idea of the greatest good, and man is thus by definition a political animal.

Needless to say, not everyone has shared the philosopher's admiration. In its advanced form, as expressed in the modern political party and the negative campaign ad, state politics impresses few. Man seems to have fallen from a political animal to a political beast.

Nothing in Excess

Young men err in everything by excess and vehemence, contrary to the precept of Chilon: they do all things too much, since they love and hate too much, and likewise in everything else. They fancy and insist that they know all things, and this is why they overdo everything.

Aristotle, *Rhetoric*, Book 2, chapter 12

Chilon was a Spartan magistrate of the sixth century B.C., whose legendary wisdom earned him a place among the Seven Sages of Greece [*see* p. 72]. Aristotle attributes the maxim "Nothing in excess" to Chilon, and it is the cornerstone of Aristotelian ethics. Elsewhere Aristotle says that "it is the nature of [activity] to be destroyed by defect and excess" (*Nicomachean Ethics*, Book 2, chapter 2). "Moderation in all things" are his watchwords [*see* THE GOLDEN MEAN].

In Aristotle's view, the nature of youth is characterized by excess, just as the nature of age is to suffer defects. Youthful hotheadedness is an excess of passion; youthful gullibility is an excess of trust; and so on. The same assumptions underlie the typical depiction of the adolescent male in Latin comedy. In Terence's *Andria*, for example, the father Simo says of his son that "What almost all young men do, applying their spirit to some endeavor, such as keeping horses or hunting-dogs, or studying philosophy, he pursued none of these things above the others, but rather all of them moderately. I rejoiced." To which his servant Sosia replies, "You were right to; for I think the chief principle in life is 'Nothing too much.'"

Peripatetic

"A Peripatetic President," runs one headline in the January 25, 1989 *New York Times*: "Election Over, He Runs." What the accompanying article, a searching piece of journalism, describes is President George Bush's now-famous decision to take an afternoon jog, reporters and photographers in tow, mere days after assuming office. This whimsical event was taken to characterize the man; according to reporter Maureen Dowd, Bush "has seemed in perpetual motion since his election."

"In perpetual motion" is a good equivalent of what we mean by "peripatetic," which ultimately derives from the Greek *peripatos*, a courtyard for walking about, and more directly from *peripatetikos*, "given to walking about" (not "given to jogging about"). This unwieldy and somewhat pretentious adjective would never have entered the language but for one very famous peripatetic philosopher: Aristotle. As the story goes, Aristotle was fond of pacing about in the *peripatos* at his Lyceum [*see* p. 100], a habit he passed on to later deep thinkers. His system of thought came to be named after this practice, and thus was born the Peripatetic School of philosophy.

All the early uses of "peripatetic" in English refer to Aristotle's teachings, but its potential as a humorous metaphor became obvious by the late sixteenth century. John Moore applied the term with gusto in 1617: "The devil is a Peripatetic . . . always walking and going about, seeking whom he may ensnare."

A Probable Impossibility

Probable impossibilities are to be preferred [in tragedy] to improbable possibilities. Plots also should not be composed from irrational parts, but as much as possible indeed should have nothing irrational in them. If, however, this is impossible, care should be taken that the irrational circumstance does not pertain to the story, as in the case of Oedipus's not knowing how Laius died.

Aristotle, *Poetics*, chapter 24

What is a "probable impossibility"? Imagine trying to make someone believe something you know is impossible—for example, that this book will not be a best-seller. Achieving this would depend on building up a case based on well-established or easily acceptable facts ("the market is whimsical"). What Aristotle means by "probable" here is "convincing" in the sense "in accordance with what has gone before."

Such a task is easier in drama than in real life. Aristotle allows that drama may portray impossible events, but he insists that good plays must convince the audience that their actions could happen in real life. To be avoided is the "improbable possibility"—something not totally out of the question, but apt to strike the audience as quite unlikely or illogical. So if a god were suddenly to appear on stage and turn the hero into a tree, the dramatist should at least make sure that the event is likely or logical within the context of the plot. If not, such events ought to be kept off the stage. Sophocles, for example, never makes an issue of the improbable, though possible, fact that King Oedipus is ignorant of how his predecessor Laius died. (If Oedipus knew, he'd already know he himself killed Laius—*see* OEDIPUS COMPLEX).

Quintessence

We must conclude that there exists a corporal substance different from the formations we find here, and that it surpasses them all in divinity as in excellence. . . . There exists, in addition to the bodies that surround us on earth, a body both different and separate, whose nature is more noble the farther it is from our own environs.

Aristotle, *On the Heavens,* Book 1, chapter 2

The philosopher Empedocles had already determined that all earthly things are composed of four elements, or essences—earth, air, fire, and water [*see* NATURE ABHORS A VACUUM *and* HARMONY IN DISCORD]. But when Aristotle observed that heavenly bodies moved in circles, this led him to rethink and expand Empedocles' theory. He deduced that there must be some fifth element—later called *quinta essentia* in Latin—which is prior to and better than the other four. This fifth element (sometimes called "ether" from the Greek *aither*) became known in English as the "quintessence," after the Latin form.

Aristotle reasoned this way: all complex motion is a combination of three elementary types of motion: upward, downward, and circular. If we assume, with Aristotle, that things move in a way that is natural to them, then their motion is determined by how they are composed. Of Empedocles' elements, earth and water tend to move downward, while fire and air tend to move upward. Since circular motion cannot be derived from a combination of upward and downward motion, there must be some fifth element which composes the heavenly bodies and makes them go round. Furthermore, since circular motion is more perfect than motion in a straight line, it must be prior to it—to Aristotle, earlier is necessarily better, and vice versa. Therefore, this fifth element is "more divine" than the other four.

Through time the term underwent gradual redefinition. In medieval chemistry it referred to the animating component of any body, as distinct from its inert matter. Modern thought took this idea a little further: the quintessence of a thing was its purest and most concentrated part, containing all its essential properties. But in popular usage, "quintessence" lost all connection with chemistry and physics, and was employed by the seventeenth century to mean simply "the most excellent example" or "the perfect embodiment." John Milton, for example, wrote in 1649 that "Lawyers say [English law] is the quintessence of reason"; and Ben Franklin noted in 1759 that "The last period [sentence] of the governor's message was the very quintessence of invective."

A Tragic Flaw

[The best kind of protagonist in tragedy] is one who neither excels in virtue and justice, nor falls through vice and depravity into misfortune after being a man of great renown and prosperity, but who has experienced this change through a certain flaw [*hamartia*]—such as Oedipus and Thyestes, and other illustrious men of this kind.

Aristotle, Poetics, chapter 13

The idea that the tragic hero must bring on his own destruction through a "tragic flaw" is more a product of modern literary criticism than a rule that the original writers of tragedy strictly observed. Aristotle makes only this one remark, and it's never been entirely clear what he means by it. Other translators have preferred to render the word *hamartia* as "mistake," "error," or "error of judgment." But in the popular view, a "tragic flaw" is a moral, not an intellectual, failing, and is innate in the character. But if *hamartia* is really a character flaw rather than an isolated bad decision, then we would be apt to think that the hero really deserves his misfortune, which Aristotle clearly states is improper.

In Aristotle's scheme, tragedies arouse "pity and fear." So certain kinds of plots are ruled out: the misfortune of an excellent man (too shocking); the good fortune of a wicked man (not satisfying); the misfortune of a bad man (we applaud). Since tragedy deals with misfortune, the hero must not, then, be a preeminently good man; but on the other hand, we can pity him only if his misfortune is undeserved. In general, then, Aristotle seems to mean by "tragic flaw" a mistake that, while not inconsistent with the hero's character, brings him more bad fortune than he really deserves.

GREEK DRAMA

We know that the Greeks invented drama, but its origins are prehistoric and thus shadowy. It is not possible to say, for example, whether comedy or tragedy developed first, though tragedy was incorporated into official city festivals at an earlier date. It does seem however that comedy grew out of the antics of reveling mimics, and tragedy out of choral lyrics devoted to heroes and gods. (The name "comedy" probably derives from the Greek for "merry-making bard"; but nobody has explained what tragedy, from the Greek for "goat song," had to do with goats.) Both forms appear to have been pioneered by the Dorian peoples of the Greek Peloponnese, in the southeastern part of the peninsula.

Ancient writers claim that formal tragedy was invented in the sixth century B.C. by Thespis [*see* THESPIAN], but the earliest complete tragedies we have are by the great poet Aeschylus (524–456 B.C.), who established his career at the Athenian festivals of Dionysus, god of wine and ecstasy. Aeschylus practically invented dramatic dialogue, since it was he who added a second actor (over and above the chorus); a third actor was later supplied by Sophocles (ca. 496–406 B.C.). Where Aeschylus wrote plays in groups, Sophocles was the first to write stand-alone tragedies, even though we think of him primarily as the author of the monumental "Theban trilogy"—*Oedipus the King, Oedipus at Colonus,* and *Antigone* (*Antigone* was probably written first). The last of the great Greek tragedians was Euripides (ca. 480–406 B.C.), a younger contemporary of Sophocles. Euripides was much more an individualist than his predecessors, and his plays, being quite melodramatic and passionate, were closer to the people.

According to tradition, the first author of formal comedy was Cratinus (ca. 520–423 B.C.), but the earliest surviving comedies are by Aristophanes (ca. 450–385 B.C.), an Athenian. Aristophanes' satiric and often bawdy plays exemplify what has become known as "Old Comedy," which flourished in the democratic environment of late fifth-century Athens. After the city was conquered by Macedonia, however, the subversive political debate and ad hominem attacks of the Old Comedy gradually gave way to the domestic foibles of anonymous characters in "New Comedy," whose greatest producer was Menander (341–290 B.C.).

Menander is noteworthy for his superior plotting, for his development of character, and for his attempt to capture everyday life as it really was. If he achieved this "realism," however, we would have to believe that the Greeks of his day were constantly falling in love with seemingly disreputable women and scheming to overcome barriers to marriage.

Most people today, when they read Greek drama in school, read tragedies, especially Sophocles'. But Menander, whose surviving work is mostly fragmentary, proved more influential in the early development of modern drama [see ROMAN DRAMA].

A Thespian

At about this time Thespis began to present his tragedies, which, because
of their rarity, delighted the people . . . . Solon, naturally curious, . . . went
one day to see Thespis, who played a part himself, as was the old custom of
the poets. After the play was over, Solon called Thespis to him and
demanded to know if he were not ashamed to lie so openly before the
world. Thespis answered that there was no substance to the things he said
or did, since all was in play. Then Solon, beating the ground with his staff,
replied, "But if we approve lying in play, we shall afterwards find earnest
lying in all our bargaining and dealing."

Plutarch, Life of Solon, chapter 29

The word "thespian," which now refers to both comic and tragic
actors, is a tribute to Thespis, a tragedian of the sixth century B.C.
There had been tragedy of a sort before Thespis; but, according
to Diogenes Laertius, "the chorus by itself played the entire
drama; later Thespis, to rest the chorus, invented one actor,
Aeschylus created a second, Sophocles a third." Thespis's
innovation must have seemed radical at the time, and the
Greeks could never bring themselves to put more than three
actors on stage.

Though Thespis's tragedies are lost, the generations have
revered him for originating the acting profession. In English,
"thespian" was at first synonymous with drama as a whole but
was narrowed to its present meaning ("actor") during the nineteenth century.

Plutarch's amusing anecdote of Solon's encounter with Thespis
incidentally illustrates the trouble actors had—and would continue to have for centuries—with the guardians of morality. The
way Solon sees it, the actor is a liar, since he pronounces untruths
"openly before the world." Like Plato after him, Solon refuses
to distinguish fictions from lies, and he thinks Thespis is only
teaching the public how to commit frauds.

Cloud-Cuckoo-Land

KORYPHAIOS   Now what shall our city be called? . . .
EUELPIDES   Something after the clouds,
        From those lofty regions in which we dwell—
        Something puffed-up and impressive.
PISTHETAIROS   How about "Cloud-cuckoo-land"?

Aristophanes, *The Birds*

"Cloud-cuckoo-land" may sound ridiculous, but no more so than its Greek equivalent *nephelokikkygia,* coined by Aristophanes in his play *The Birds* (414 B.C.). The characters Pisthetairos ("Hopeful") and Euelpides ("Plausible"), fed up with the hustle and bustle of Athens, are on the perennial quest for a better life in more attractive environs. No other place on earth satisfies them, so they decide to build an ideal city in the sky. Though the avian natives are skeptical at first, they soon agree to help these dreamers. The first thing to do, of course, is come up with a name for the place; Pisthetairos, inspired, submits "Cloud-cuckoo-land," and thus is born an epithet for all future castles in the air.

As you might expect, things turn out rather badly in the new utopia. All the pernicious characters the Athenians had hoped to escape wind up back on their doorstep—beggarly poets, astrologers, informers, mischievous gods, etc. The failure of so grand a project served nicely as a metaphor for former British prime minister Margaret Thatcher, who once accused the other leaders of the European Community of living in "cloud-cuckoo-land." The British seem fonder of the epithet than are Americans, who prefer the abbreviation "cloudland."

The Riddle of the Sphinx

Now, Teiresias, give us one case when you
Have seen clearly. When the Sphinx was here,
Who sang us dark riddles, how come you found no answer
To deliver the citizens of Thebes? To be sure, an answer
Was not available to the first who came.
. . . Then I, Oedipus, presented myself,
Who was ignorant; I consulted no augur, but
By a simple effort of reflection silenced the Sphinx.

Sophocles, *Oedipus the King,* lines 390–394, 397–398

The Sphinx is first mentioned in Greek literature by Hesiod, who describes it only as "deadly" and refers to it as a "he." But as we know from surviving Greek art, the sphinxes imagined by Hesiod's contemporaries were almost exclusively female. It is true, however, that the older Egyptian sphinxes were male—in fact, they were portrait statues of pharaohs, with the king's head stuck on a lion's body. (The oldest surviving sphinx, at Giza in Egypt, dates to the reign of the Pharaoh Khafre, ca. 2550 B.C.) The Greeks added wings when, circa 1600 B.C., they modeled their sphinxes on Asian samples, which were also generally female.

According to the legend Sophocles refers to here, a sphinx was sent to Thebes by Hera, queen of the gods. Like other such divine "gifts," the Sphinx turned out to be a monstrous bane, gobbling up everyone who failed to solve her riddle. This riddle has come down in several versions, but basically it went like this: "What goes on four legs in the morning, two legs at noon, and three legs in the evening?" This stumped even the blind prophet Teiresias, who was at least smart enough to avoid venturing an answer.

Oedipus was no prophet, but he cracked the conundrum. The answer, obviously, is "man"—who crawls at birth ("morning"), walks upright at maturity ("noon"), and employs a cane in old age ("evening"). According to some accounts, the Sphinx was so vexed by Oedipus's success that she committed suicide. Oedipus, on the other hand, was made king of Thebes for the deed, and was given Queen Jocasta's hand in marriage. This seems well and good on the surface, but it will turn out that Jocasta is Oedipus's mother.

In this scene, Teiresias has just revealed what Oedipus still refuses to accept: that the king killed his own father [see OEDIPUS COMPLEX]. In a fit of tragic hubris, Oedipus boasts of his triumph over the Sphinx and attempts to discredit the prophet. If you're so smart, says Oedipus, why couldn't you solve the riddle of the Sphinx?

Though in Hesiod's account the Sphinx is a monster, it later became, perhaps on account of the legend of the riddling sphinx of Thebes, a figure of obscure wisdom and divine justice. Sophocles' sphinx retains the monstrosity of Hesiod's myth; compare Berowne's puzzling, but hardly frightening, version in Shakespeare's *Love's Labor's Lost*, where love is described as "Subtle as Sphinx, as sweet and musical/ As bright Apollo's lute" (Act 4, scene 3).

The Oedipus Complex

Then, without my parents' knowledge, I went to Pytho.
But Phoebus refused to answer my question;
He dismissed me, but not before predicting
All sorts of horrors and calamities: that I would marry
My mother, that I would beget a monstrous posterity,
Horrible in men's eyes, and finally that I would become
The murderer of my own father.

Sophocles, *Oedipus the King*, lines 787–793

Anyone with a glancing knowledge of the works of Sigmund Freud is familiar with the Oedipus complex. But in Sophocles' tragedy *Oedipus the King,* which Freud cited, Oedipus doesn't really have an Oedipus complex at all. In fact, his feelings and psychology have almost nothing to do with the tragic events of the play. Rather, his story demonstrates that we are putty in the hands of fate, and that it is foolish to try avoiding what must be. Oedipus doesn't *wish* to kill his father and marry his mother—that's the destiny he vainly attempts to escape.

Freud "discovered" his version of the Oedipus complex after putting himself through self-analysis. In 1897 he wrote to a colleague that "we can understand the riveting power of *Oedipus Rex*" because the "Greek legend seizes on a compulsion which everyone recognizes because he feels it within himself." What Freud saw in himself was an intense love for his mother and a consequent jealousy of his father; and he recalled childhood fantasies of putting the latter out of the picture. Since such feelings superficially match the events of Sophocles' tragedy, Freud coined the term "Oedipus complex" (*Ödipuskomplex*) to describe them, and committed the phrase to writing in his 1910 essay "A Special Type of Object Choice Made by Men." (It's always the *Oedipus* complex; *oedipal* is a stand-alone adjective.)

The original story begins when, as prince of Corinth, Oedipus is accused by a drunkard of being King Polybus's illegitimate son. Though the king reassures the prince, a troubled Oedipus resorts to the oracle at Pytho, later known as Delphi [*see* p. 33]. The oracle evades the issue of whether Oedipus is legitimate or not, but delivers the terrible news that the prince is fated to murder his father and lie with his mother. Naturally enough, Oedipus has no intention of letting this happen, so he flees Corinth for Thebes.

But here's the rub: at a certain crossroads, Oedipus meets a herald and carriage. When the herald gets rough and tries to push Oedipus off the road, the hot-headed prince starts a fight and subsequently kills everybody involved. Unfortunately, one of the men in the carriage is his natural father, King Laius of Thebes. After solving the riddle of the Sphinx and thus saving Thebes from its pest [*see* p. 112], Oedipus is made king and marries the widowed queen Jocasta—his natural mother. Only later, when a plague descends on Thebes, to be lifted when the murderer of Laius is identified and expelled, do the facts come out. Oedipus doesn't take it well and puts out his own eyes.

Before Oedipus decided that he could escape the oracle's prophecy, his victim Laius had made the same mistake. When Apollo predicts that his son will kill him, Laius has a spike driven through one of the infant Oedipus's feet and has the child exposed on a mountain. But the boy is found and brought to King Polybus, who adopts him. Thus the source of Oedipus's confusion, and thus his name: "*oidipous*" means "swell-foot."

Well, Carl Jung didn't have a swollen foot, but Freud might well have accused him of having an Oedipus complex. The younger psychoanalyst, a protégé of Freud, ended up breaking with his mentor and repudiating much of his teaching. One of the things they argued about was the difference between boys' and girls' sexual development.

Freud's Oedipus complex describes a phase of the little boy's psychological growth, but he initially assumed it was equally applicable to little girls. He later changed his mind, however, and while he still claimed there was a female Oedipus complex, he argued that it was a very different thing altogether from the male version. Jung, meanwhile, proposed that the girl's development precisely mirrored the boy's, and coined in 1913 the term "Electra complex" to describe the female version.

Jung also turned to Greek tragedy, specifically to the several versions of the story of Electra. In Aeschylus's *The Libation Bearers* (458 B.C.), Electra, prompted by the god Apollo, collaborates with her brother to do in their mother Clytaemestra, who was responsible for their father's death. Jung probably had Sophocles' version, *Electra* (ca. 418 B.C.), chiefly in mind, for it is there that Electra takes the principal role in plotting vengeance. Though not as raw or suggestive as his depiction of Oedipus, Sophocles' version of Electra, as a woman deeply attached to her father and impelled to murder her mother, served Jung quite nicely as an analogue.

Better Never to Have Been Born

CHORUS Never to have been born is best;
    But if we must see the light, the next best
    Is quickly returning whence we came.
    When youth departs, with all its follies,
    Who does not stagger under evils? Who escapes them?

Sophocles, Oedipus at Colonus, lines 1224–1231

The petulant cry of the disappointed child—"I wish I had never been born!"—was one of ancient Greece's standard truths, most memorably expressed by the chorus of Sophocles' rather depressing play *Oedipus at Colonus* (401 B.C.). Actually, these elderly gentlemen look back fondly upon their carefree youth. The recent troubles of Oedipus, however, convince them that a fun-filled childhood can never compensate for painful maturity.

Not only is Oedipus blind and banished from Thebes, where until lately he was king [*see* OEDIPUS COMPLEX]; furthermore, he has become a pariah at Colonus, his sons are fighting over the Theban crown, and Creon, who is currently ruling Thebes, has just tried to capture Oedipus and his two daughters. The gods apparently deserted Oedipus long ago—even at the moment he was born; and this, the chorus points out, is a not uncommon fate.

This haunting choral song inspired at least two of the great modern poets. William Butler Yeats freely translated it as "From *Oedipus at Colonus*," part of "A Man Young and Old." W. H. Auden recalls the phrase in his more whimsical "Death's Echo": "The desires of the heart are as crooked as corkscrews,/ Not to be born is the best for man;/ The second-best is a formal order,/ The dance's pattern; dance while you can." Where Oedipus is tortured by the gods, Auden's subject is tortured by desire, and spoiled children are tortured by parental restraints.

Nothing Is More Wonderful Than Man

CHORUS Of so many marvelous things, nothing
Is more wonderful than man; he crosses the foamy sea
In the south wind, navigating its depths and crests;
And the mother of gods, the sovereign Earth, immortal,
Inexhaustible, year after year he takes his plow
And furrows her with horse and mule.

Sophocles, *Antigone*, lines 332–341

Very sweet; but let's get this thing in context. At this moment in Sophocles' *Antigone*, King Creon of Thebes has just been told that someone has violated his order that the corpse of Oedipus's son Polynices be left to rot in the sun. Creon detects the work of "stiff-necked anarchists" and flies into a rage, threatening to hang anyone who doesn't cooperate in finding the perpetrator. (The perpetrator turns out to be Polynices' sister Antigone.)

So what the chorus is getting at here is a little hard to figure out. They begin by praising man's power and industry, but end up singing darkly of the dire fate of those who violate the law. Do they mean the law of the gods—which Creon violates by dishonoring the corpse—or do they mean the law of Creon—which Antigone has violated? This chorus is uncharacteristically unhelpful. Later events do clarify the moral, since when Creon ultimately causes Antigone's suicide, he is punished with the deaths of his son and wife.

So is nothing more wonderful than man? That's not the message of Sophocles' play, which rather seems to be that doom awaits those who defy the gods. We've adopted a few lines that seem quite upbeat, but perhaps by the phrase we translate as "wonderful" Sophocles meant something more like "strange."

To Leave No Stone Unturned

Though I was rid of Hercules, I knew
I was hated by his children, and the feud
Would continue, so I left no stone unturned
To find the scorpions underneath; I plotted
To kill or banish them, to assure my safety.

Euripides, The Children of Hercules, lines 1000–1004

It's pretty difficult to keep the details of Hercules' life and
exploits straight, especially since every Greek author has a
different version. But most of them agree that Zeus fathered
Hercules by the mortal Alcmena, and that the god's wife Hera
thus developed a life-long hatred of Alcmena's illegitimate son.
After the oracle at Delphi [*see* p. 33] informed Hercules that he
could win immortality by serving his cousin King Eurystheus of
Tiryns for twelve years, Hera inspired the king to devise a series
of deadly labors. Hercules survives these trials but eventually
dies anyway.

In Euripides' version of consequent events, Eurystheus,
fearing retribution from Hercules' children, plots their death.
The Heraclidae, as they were known, flee to Athens; Eurystheus
declares war on the city, but is defeated, captured, and brought
before Hercules' mother Alcmena, who spends the rest of the
play cursing him. In the passage I have quoted, Eurystheus
justifies himself on the grounds of self-defense, and claims that
he was forced to "leave no stone unturned" in his search for the
"scorpions" who were presumably out for revenge.

Euripides' expression "to leave no stone unturned" quickly
became a catch-phrase among the Greeks and later the Romans.
When the younger Pliny wrote a letter to his friend, the historian
Tacitus, he even quoted the phrase in Greek, a sure testimony
to its familiarity, at least among the well-read in Rome.

To Call a Spade a Spade

I am the god Argument, friend of free speech and truth, enemy only to those who fear my frankness. I know all and speak what I know, whether it be good or evil; I call a fig a fig and a kneading-trough a kneading-trough.

Menander, unidentified fragment

Calling a spade a spade is the very epitome of straightforwardness, both in its form and in its meaning. But if not for a small slip of a Renaissance translator, we would be busily calling "a kneading-trough a kneading-trough." (A kneading-trough is a wooden tub built for that purpose.)

In this fragment, Menander's character Argument, god of frankness, turns a line from Aristophanes' play *The Clouds* ("What is a trough he calls a trough") into a much-quoted Greek proverb. The Greek satirist Lucian and the Latin rhetorician Cicero, for example, both quote Menander, and the amusing metaphor later showed up in several books of proverbs—such as Plutarch's *Apophthegms*—and even in elementary grammar books. (Plutarch also attributes the saying to Philip II of Macedon.)

Englishmen, however, were not so familiar with the fig, and "kneading-trough" lacks the brevity that makes for a good catch-phrase. "Spade" fits the bill on the counts of familiarity and brevity, but so do a lot of other words. We owe the choice of "spade" to the Dutch humanist Erasmus, who (perhaps knowingly) mistranslated Plutarch, substituting the Latin *ligo* ("hoe" or "spade") for the Greek "kneading-trough." (The two words are nearly identical in Greek.) And thus when Nicholas Udall translated Erasmus's version into English in 1542, he rendered it "to call a spade . . . a spade." By this tortuous path—from Aristophanes to Menander to Plutarch to Erasmus to Udall— was coined a phrase.

A Deus ex Machina

You are by your epiphany a veritable "god from the machine."

Menander, *The Woman Possessed with a Divinity*, fragment

Deus ex machina is one of those Latin phrases more familiar in the original than in translation—"a god from the machine." This is probably because the English word "machine" is reserved for such devices as your washer and dryer, while the Latin *machina*, derived from Menander's *mechane*, plays on several meanings.

In its original version, the Greek *mechane* really meant "machine." When dramatists brought a god on stage, they set him down with a hand-operated crane, expecting this would produce the desired effect of awe. The critics, however, were not impressed. This practice was frowned upon by Plato, for example, who scoffed at tragic poets "who in any perplexity have their gods waiting in the air" (*Cratylus*). And Mr. Criticism himself, Aristotle, insisted in his *Poetics* that "the dénouements of plots should come out of the characters, and not from the 'machine.'"

Given the gist of Aristotle's criticism, *deus ex machina* came to refer not to any particular god in any particular machine, but rather to the artificial resolution—the miraculous intervention of some unlooked-for event or personage. The Latin *machina* reflects this sense, since it also came to mean a poet's "machine"—his artifice. Nobody recognizes the pun anymore, and so we use *deus ex machina* only in its late sense, to mean any obviously rigged resolution to a literary plot or real-life dilemma.

Roman Drama

The origins of Latin drama, like those of Greek drama [*see* p. 108], are obscure. In all likelihood, Roman comedy and tragedy evolved, like the Greek versions, out of native satire and lyric; but when it came to giving these performances dramatic structure, the Romans did what came naturally: they stole from the Greeks.

The first authentic dramatist in Rome seems to have been Livius Andronicus, actually a Greek, who presented Latin versions of Greek plays at an official religious festival in 240 B.C. Dramatists from then on adapted characters, situations, and plots directly from Greek sources, with a few exceptions—the Romans did invent the history play.

Though there were many earlier forays into tragic and comic drama, the Latin theater came into its own with the comedies of Plautus (ca. 254–184 B.C.), who is said to have written 130 plays (only 21 survived the purge of Marcus Varro, a friend of Cicero, who rejected the rest as spurious). Plautus specialized in adapting Greek New Comedies [*see* p. 109], most of which are set in Athens at some indeterminate time, and all of which are in the spirit of contemporary Roman life. Plautus was succeeded by the less prolific but more polished comedian Terence (ca. 195–159 B.C.). Terence, born at Carthage and brought to Rome as a slave, mined the same field as Plautus, but lacked his predecessor's taste for burlesque and occasional brutality.

Latin comedy is distinctively superior to Latin tragedy, and the Romans produced only one tragedian whose works had any impact on later drama. He was Seneca the Younger (4 B.C.–A.D. 65), who, like his comic counterparts, drew on Greek originals, but whose nine or ten adaptations are too clever and labored by half. Yet these works, which seem to have been closet dramas, did play an important role in the development of English tragedy in the later sixteenth century, though their influence falls well short of that of Latin comedy. Much that is great in Renaissance comedies, both Italian and English, derives from Plautus and Terence; very little of what is great in Renaissance tragedies, such as Shakespeare's, owes much to Seneca.

So while enlightened opinion, from Aristotle to the present, has taken Greek tragedies, Sophocles' in particular, to be the pinnacle of dramatic art, Greek comedy played a bigger role in the development of the Roman and later of the European drama. Menander may be virtually unknown today, and Plautus and Terence almost as obscure, but we can still find their footprints in the average situation comedy.

Eyes in the Back of Your Head

I know for sure that I've never seen anyone more wicked
Than this old hag; and I'm awfully afraid that,
With some plot, she'll catch me unawares
And detect the gold where it's hidden;
She has eyes even in the back of her head, the wretch.

Plautus, *The Pot of Gold*, Act 1, scene 1, lines 60–64

The old man Euclio, who has discovered a pile of gold hidden in his house, is determined to keep it hidden. Yet he's bedeviled by the paranoid fantasy that everyone he meets somehow already knows about his loot and is plotting to make off with it. He's especially suspicious of his trusty, if dim, servant Straphyla, the "old hag" he accuses in this speech; according to Euclio, she "has eyes even in the back of her head."

Plautus's phrase, now a popular metaphor for someone with uncanny powers of detection, is related to dozens of common phrases equating eyes with penetration. The link of seeing to knowledge is especially strong in classical thought—our word "theory," for example, derives from the Greek word for "spectator." The equation is also found in Western religious thought; "I have sinned in the eyes of God," the trespasser confesses, meaning "God has penetrated to my soul and the filthiness thereof cannot escape him." Eyes are wonderful organs, but like Euclio, we sometimes wish others didn't have so many.

Water from a Stone

TOXILUS You can make me your everlasting friend .
SAGARISTO   How?
TOXILUS By giving me sixty silver coins so that I may buy her freedom,
    Which I will pay back immediately, in three days' time, or four.
    Be a true friend and help me out.
SAGARISTO What arrogance, to dare asking me for so much money!
    Even if I sold my whole self, I would scarcely get enough
    To cover it. You're asking for water from a pumice stone,
    That's thirsty itself.

Plautus, *The Persian*, Act 1, scene 1, lines 37–42

The slave Toxilus finds himself in a familiar situation: in love, but flat broke. But his problem isn't that he can't afford to take his sweetheart out to a nice restaurant; rather, if he wants her at all, he's got to buy her from her current owner—she, too, is a slave. Welcome to Rome, second century B.C. Toxilus tries hitting up his fellow slave Sagaristo for the necessary funds, but the latter protests that he couldn't even sell himself for the sum Toxilus requires. As Sagaristo says, Toxilus asks for "water from a pumice-stone," a notoriously dry, granite-like specimen.

Sagaristo's jest became proverbial for vain pursuits. But in English quotations, dating from about 1580, other stones (flint, for example) were substituted for pumice, a volcanic product not often found in the English countryside. Charles Dickens so intensified the metaphor that his version became more familiar than the original: "Blood cannot be obtained from a stone, neither can anything on account be obtained ... from Mr. Micawber" (*David Copperfield*, 1850).

A Word to the Wise

SATURIO Here I am! Hope I didn't keep you waiting.
TOXILUS Go on, get over there far off and out of sight, and be silent;
   When you see me talking to the pimp—
SATURIO A word to the wise is enough.
TOXILUS Then, when I've gone—
SATURIO Why don't you be quiet? I know what you want.

Plautus, The Persian, Act 4, scene 7, lines 726–729

The clever slave Toxilus, whom we have met before [*see* WATER FROM A STONE], has successfully cheated one of the local pimps, and here he instructs his co-conspirator Saturio on the next phase of their plan. Toxilus wants Saturio to keep his mouth shut; the latter bristles at Toxilus's instructions, indignantly insisting that he knows exactly what to do and doesn't need to be told twice. "A word to the wise is enough," he quips. Of course, he doesn't keep his mouth shut, and reveals all to the pimp.

Saturio's come-back—*dictum sapienti sat est*—already sounds like a proverb in his mouth (honest), but it's the first record we have of the phrase. A slightly modified version—*verbum sapienti sat est*, which translates identically—became so famous that it was no longer necessary to quote the whole thing; *verbum sap.*— even *verb. sap.*— did the trick. Similarly, the English rendering, first found in the 1570s, was quickly replaced by a more familiar abbreviation, as, for example, in Ben Jonson's play *The Case Is Altered* (1590s): "Go to, a word to the wise." But as the short form became more familiar than the original, its meaning subtly altered. "A word to the wise" no longer means "a few words are sufficient to warn the intelligent," but rather "if you are wise, you will listen to what I tell you."

Whom the Gods Love Dies Young

CHRYSALUS   Whom the gods love
Dies young; yet he lives—breathes—is conscious.
If any god loved this man, he should have died
More than ten, no, more than twenty years ago.
He burdens the ground as he walks, already senseless
And witless, worth about as much as a stinking mushroom.

Plautus, *The Two Bacchises*, Act 4, scene 7, lines 816–821

Like any slave worth his salt in Latin comedy, Plautus's Chrysalus is impudent at every opportunity. Here he gets away with insulting his master because he has some information he knows the old man is dying for. (This "information" is just a ruse.) His little joke is based on the proverb, "Whom the gods love dies young," which seems to originate in the Greek play *The Double Deceiver*, by Menander, on which Plautus based *The Two Bacchises*. A slave speaks the line in Menander, too; but whether he was as ironic as Chrysalus we don't know. The original is lost, though Menander's line shows up in classical quote-books.

Menander wasn't the first to express the idea that "only the good die young," but his version, directly cited in English by 1546, impressed many famous English authors. John Dryden quotes it in "The Hind and the Panther" (1687), as does Lord Byron in *Don Juan* (1819–1824). (Byron had already written "Heaven gives its favorites early death" in *Childe Harold's Pilgrimage* [1809–1818]. Quoting Menander was an improvement.) Some authors substituted "God" for "gods," but now the pagan version seems more natural—everybody seems to know they're quoting the classics, even if they don't know which one.

Fortune Favors the Brave

PHAEDRIA What are you saying?
GETA   That I saw his father, your uncle.
ANTIPHO Wretched me! How can I find a remedy for this sudden ruin?
   For if it is my fortune, Phanium, to be divided from you,
   Life is no longer desirable to me.
GETA   Now that it is so, Antipho,
   So much the more ought you be watchful: fortune favors the brave.

Terence, *Phormio*, Act 1, scene 3, lines 199–203

The young Antipho finds himself in love with a woman his father wouldn't approve of—a typical dilemma for young men in Latin comedy. And, as usual, the father is about to discover the facts, and so the lover begs his witty slave to scheme their way out of disaster. The scenario is completely predictable—a fact Terence would readily have acknowledged; as he says elsewhere, "nothing is said that has not been said before" [*see* p. 129].

The slave Geta's inspirational catch-phrase, "Fortune favors the brave," had been said before too, by the Greek poet Simonides (fifth century B.C.), but Terence's version is the one people remembered, at least for a while. Virgil employed it in the *Aeneid*, but with a twist; instead of "brave," he says "bold." The later version was apparently more familiar to English writers, at least before the nineteenth century—Terence was drilled into every schoolboy's head, but so was Virgil.

The most famous version of the idea isn't Virgil's, or Terence's, but rather Machiavelli's. As had his predecessors, the Italian depicted Fortune as a goddess (now known as "Lady Luck"), who, like any woman, "allows herself more often to be mastered" by the bold, bullying man "than by those who approach her coldly" (*The Prince*). Though Machiavelli's sexist metaphor has disintegrated with time, we still hear tell that fortune favors the brave.

Nothing Is Said That Has Not Been Said Before

He doesn't deny that in his *Eunuch* he has transported characters out of the Greek; but . . . if the same characters will not be permitted, how is it more permissible to depict a servant on the run, or to make use of good old women, evil courtesans, a gluttonous parasite, a braggart soldier, a changeling, an old man duped by a servant, or even love, hate, and suspicion? In short, nothing is said that has not been said before.

Terence, *The Eunuch*, Prologue, lines 31–41

It is a corollary of Ecclesiastes' tenet, "there is no new thing under the sun" (1:9), that there are no new ideas either. The Latin dramatist Terence said as much circa 160 B.C. in the prologue to his comedy *The Eunuch*. Terence used prologues to refute the critics, who in this case accused him, at a private preview, of having plundered Plautus's play *The Flatterer* (now lost) for his plot.

Well, replied Terence, if you really want to know, Plautus stole *his* plot from the Greek dramatist Menander. So where are you going to draw the line? Every Latin comedy recycles a limited set of character-types—frantic slave, greedy parasite, and so on—so you'd pretty much have to abolish the form if you wanted to outlaw borrowing. And how about love, hate, and jealousy? Are they off-limits because other playwrights have already treated them? Terence aims at a *reductio ad absurdum;* the end-point of his demonstration is that "nothing is said that has not been said before" (which is why you're reading this book). Though he perhaps exaggerates, the point is valid enough, much to the chagrin of any practicing writer.

Thrasonical

THRASO   I have a certain gift
  Which indeed makes everything I do pleasing.
GNATHO By Hercules, I've marked that spirit in you.
THRASO So the king always gave me the greatest thanks
  For whatever I did: he praised no one else so much.
GNATHO Often, a man may, with a few words, transfer to himself
  All the glory others have earned with their labor—
  That is, if he has wit, which you certainly do.
THRASO Of course.

Terence, *The Eunuch*, Act 3, scene 1, lines 395–401

Terence's character Thraso is the best-known representative of a stock comic type, the braggart warrior. Though a coward and a weakling, Thraso, like all his kin, is an incorrigible promoter of his own virtues, boasting of military prowess, royal favor, and animal magnetism. In this scene, Thraso, seconded by his "parasite" Gnatho, basks in the supposed favor of his courtesan as well as of the king. Yet he is too dull-witted to detect the irony of Gnatho's replies.

Thraso became so famous for this vainglory that he lent his name to a common adjective for it: "thrasonical." The word entered English by way of a 1564 translation by Miles Coverdale, better known as one of the early translators of the Bible. Later, Shakespeare's Rosalind refers to "Caesar's thrasonical brag of I came, I saw, I overcame" (*As You Like It*, Act 5, scene 2; *see* p. 176).

Actually, Thraso is a rather mild representative of the type. More outrageous is Plautus's Pyrgopolinices, from the earlier *Braggart Warrior*. But can you imagine saying "pyrgopolinical" rather than "thrasonical"?

CICERO

(106–43 B.C.)

Anyone who's made it to second-year Latin is liable to wince at any mention of the name "Cicero." But while his famous cry "*O tempora, o mores!*" ("O, the times! O the mores!") is now an inside joke to these unfortunates, Marcus Tullius Cicero was once the centerpiece of classical education in Europe. More than Aristotle or Horace, his closest competitors in the canon, Cicero defined for the modern world its ethical and rhetorical ideals.

Though Cicero's glory among philosophers is merely reflected—he popularized the Greek peripatetic, skeptical, and stoic schools of thought rather than inventing his own—he does have a major claim to power if not originality in his rhetorical theory and speeches. The son of a Roman knight, Cicero first made his mark as a pleader in the law-courts, and then as a public speaker. He was elected consul—one of the two chief Roman magistrates—in 64 B.C., and in this office he achieved everlasting fame by foiling a conspiracy spearheaded by the rebel Catiline.

Though somewhat arrogant and thus less than popular, Cicero was a staunch defender of the Roman constitution against what he saw as dangerous tendencies toward dictatorship. This put him on the bad side of Julius Caesar, who alternately humiliated him and restored him to favor. After Caesar's assassination, however, Cicero became reckless in his opposition to Marc Antony, whom he saw as potentially a much worse tyrant than Caesar had ever been [*see* ALL IN THE SAME BOAT].

All in the Same Boat

Therefore, dear Quintus, come aboard with us, even at the helm! There is one boat now for all good citizens, which in truth we take pains to hold on its course. May our voyage prosper! But whatever winds there be, we shall certainly not lack skill. For what else can virtue assure?

Cicero, *Letters to His Friends*, Book 12, letter 25a

Cicero is writing in March of 43 B.C. to his friend Quintus Cornificius, governor of Africa Vetus ("Old Africa"), a province of the Roman Republic. He invites Quintus onto the one boat in which all Roman patriots now find themselves—the boat that sails against the swelling tyranny of Marc Antony. With Julius Caesar now dead [*see* ET TU, BRUTE?], Cicero, one of Caesar's opponents, is back in political grace, and he means to prevent Antony from becoming another Caesar—another enemy to the traditional Roman liberties.

Cicero's expression, "There is one boat now for all patriots," though worded differently, seems the ultimate source of the English phrase "All in the same boat." (Cicero may owe something to the Greek expression "all rowing together.") Little did he know how apt his phrasing would appear in retrospect. When you say that "we're all in the same boat," you usually mean that the boat is in trouble. Cicero was optimistic, but he was sailing a treacherous course. In the end, Antony joined forces with Cicero's hero, Octavius, and turned his wrath on his enemy. Antony had Cicero executed that December, and displayed his severed head and hands in the Forum. Cicero's boat was sunk.

A Friend in Need

Consider how grave, how difficult for the majority it appears to associate with calamity, and how difficult it is to find those who will fall with you. So Ennius is right: "uncertain times distinguish the certain friend." Most people stand accused of inconstancy and weakness—for slighting you in good times and deserting you in bad.

Cicero, *Of Friendship*, chapter 17, paragraph 64

Cicero's *Of Friendship* (44 B.C.), written the year before his death, has always been one of his most admired works, thanks to its stylish treatment of so common and practical a topic. As Cicero describes it, speaking in the guise of Laelius (a consul of the second century B.C.), friendship is the truest comfort of mankind; yet it must be pursued judiciously and worked at diligently. The key to friendship is virtue, by which Cicero means "goodness," "reason," and "effort." But of course, these things may be feigned; and false friends are separated from true when the chips are down. Cicero quotes the father of Latin literature, Ennius: "uncertain times distinguish the certain friend."

Ennius's aphorism is the ancestor of our cliché, "A friend in need is a friend indeed." The idea may be traced back to the earliest English literature, but the modern phrasing seems to have first appeared in a poem sometimes attributed to Shakespeare, but known to be by one Richard Barnfield: "He that is thy friend indeed,/ He will help thee in thy need." By the late seventeenth century, the expression had become proverbial.

A Sword of Damocles

Now when a certain one of Dionysius's flatterers, Damocles, praised at great length his troops, riches, majesty of rule, abundance of things, and magnificent palaces, and denied that anyone had ever been happier than he, Dionysius replied: "Do you wish, then, O Damocles, seeing that this life so charms you, to have a taste of it and to know my fortune by experience?" When Damocles said that he did indeed desire this, Dionysius ordered that he be set on a couch of gold covered with very beautiful, magnificently ornamented woven fabrics, and had him presented with several tables of engraved silver and gold plate. . . . Damocles felt himself fortunate indeed. But in the middle of this Dionysius ordered that a shining sword be suspended from the ceiling by a horse-hair, so that it hung over the shoulders of this happy man. Thus Damocles observed neither his beautiful servants nor the silver so artfully engraved, nor did he reach out his hand to the table; and at last he pulled off his crown and begged the tyrant to let him go, because now he had no desire to be happy.

Cicero, *Tusculan Disputations*, Book 5, chapter 21

Dionysius I, tyrant of Syracuse in the early fourth century B.C., was a very imaginative man—a little too imaginative for his own good. According to Cicero, though Dionysius had complete control over a rich and bountiful country, he could never really enjoy it; recognizing the injustice of his own tyrannical ways, Dionysius suffered a guilt-induced paranoia. He wouldn't even allow a barber to shave his beard, entrusting the task to his daughters; and when they were old enough to consider other uses for the blade, he had them singe his hair and beard with hot walnuts. Constantly fearful even of his own bodyguards, Dionysius built a trench around his bedchamber, and drew up the little wooden bridge after retiring for the night. Avoiding public platforms, he instead addressed his people from a tower. The stories go on.

I suppose you can never be too careful, especially if you're a tyrant; but to the less insane observer Dionysius's paranoia might be hard to understand. So when the flatterer Damocles tries to ingratiate himself by loudly proclaiming the despot's happiness, Dionysius decides to teach him how it really feels. The tyrant arrays Damocles with rich appointments, sumptuous foods, and handsome attendants, much to the flatterer's delight. But then Dionysius supplies the crowning touch: a whetted sword suspended by a horse-hair over Damocles' neck. The torture works exquisitely: Damocles can think of nothing else but his impending doom; Dionysius's bounty in fact only mocks him. So presently he begs to be released, declaring that he has no desire to be so happy.

From this amusing tale we have directly derived the phrase "a sword of Damocles" —a metaphor for a blow that might fall at any moment, a threat that robs us of any delight in our present safety. This tale is also the source of our phrase "to hang by a hair," which derives from Erasmus's retelling. ("To hang by a thread" shows up in Latin long before Cicero's *Tuscan Disputations*—Ennius employs it in his *Annals* [ca. 180 B.C.], where it has nothing to do with Damocles.) But today what "hangs by a hair" or even by a thread is not the instrument of our doom, but rather the means of our security or happiness.

Let the Punishment Fit the Crime

Since the laws must be enacted in courts as well as in words, let me add: let the punishment fit the crime, so that everyone suffers according to his vice. Violence shall be punished by exile or death, avarice by fines, and greed for honor by ignominy.

Cicero, *Laws*, Book 3, chapter 20

In this sequel to his *Republic*, which had adapted Plato's philosophy to the more pragmatic culture of Rome, Cicero concerns himself with ideal laws for an ideal commonwealth. His watchwords are "let the punishment fit the crime," essentially a slightly less harsh version of the Bible's "an eye for an eye, a tooth for a tooth." The miscreant ought to be treated in a way that is symbolically appropriate to his offense—the violent man put to death, the ambitious man disgraced, and so on.

Obviously, this notion has not been confined to philosophical utopias—it has seemed to most peoples at most times the essence of justice. Dante, for example, imagines hell and purgatory as places where sinners are punished in the image of their crimes. The most horrifying example is that of Ugolino and the Archbishop of Ruggieri, in canto 33 of the *Inferno*. In life they were political enemies, both of them treacherous, and the archbishop had arranged Ugolino's death by starvation. Now both are in the ninth circle of hell, and Ugolino is condemned to eat the archbishop's head for eternity.

Poetic License

Uncommon words are generally antiquities and archaisms, which have long since passed out of use in everyday discourse. They are more freely admitted to the license of poets than to us; yet sometimes the poetic word lends dignity to an oration, if used rarely.

Cicero, *Of the Orator,* Book 3

On reflection, it's no surprise that the original "poetic license" was issued by a lawyer. Though he dabbled in philosophy and was famous as an orator, Cicero was certainly no poet—and only non-poets talk about "poetic license." His main point here is that archaic words and neologisms (like "outbosom") are best left to the poets and ought to be only rarely employed when arguing before a jury or an assembly. Words that would sound ridiculous in everyday speech or in a court of law we condescend to appreciate in poetry, at least if they're well used. Poets are given special license to apply strange language when they aim at whipping up passion or mystery—the sorts of things we don't experience every day.

Thus Cicero meant by "poetic license" a certain freedom with diction. Likewise, the earliest uses of the phrase in English refer to tampering with poetic technique—diction, meter, metaphors, and so forth. Yet today we usually use "poetic license" to mean, not a violation of poetic rules, but the poet's freedom to tamper with fact or probability (as Pliny the Younger said, "Poets are permitted to lie"). And thus the phrase can also characterize a non-poet's taking suspicious liberties with the facts. These meanings developed only in the present century, which is not surprising; few people read poetry any more, and even fewer bother with laws of diction and meter.

VIRGIL

(70–19 B.C.)

Publius Vergilius Maro, born at Mantua, set out to be the Homer of the Roman Empire. His most famous work is the epic poem *Aeneis*, to which Virgil dedicated the last ten years of his life, while living near Naples. The *Aeneid*—as we now call it—looks to Homer in style and structure, but picks up a different strand of the Trojan War story in order to weave a nationalistic epic. Virgil follows the adventures of Aeneas, a Trojan hero and the son of Venus, as he escapes the destruction of Troy and makes his odyssey to Italy. According to Virgil's version of the legend, Aeneas, after subduing the native Latins, prepares the ground for the founding of Rome.

Though the *Aeneid* is Virgil's masterpiece, he has also left us a number of minor works which are the sources of some familiar English phrases. His authorship of "Moretum" [see p. 139] is doubtful, but the collection of *Eclogues* and the *Georgics* are genuine and important works. The ten eclogues that make up Virgil's first published work are lyric poems "sung" by fictional Sicilian shepherds, who make veiled references to political and personal events. The *Georgics* is one poem in four books or divisions; it retails loads of practical advice for the farmer, the breeder of animals, and the bee-keeper.

Virgil himself seems to have been a land-owner and to have made some money by bee-keeping, but he did much better for himself as a poet. Like Horace after him [see p. 143], he became a favorite of the wealthy patron Maecenas and of the emperor Augustus, who commanded performances of the *Aeneid* as it was being written. Augustus was so impressed by the poem that he ordered Virgil's executors to ignore the poet's wish to have the manuscript burned if he left it unfinished.

E Pluribus Unum

The right hand first mashes the fragrant garlic with a pestle,
Then grinds everything equally in a juicy mixture.
The hand goes in circles: gradually the separate essences
Lose distinction, the color is out of many one,
Neither all green, since milky-white bits resist it,
Nor shining milky white, since the herbs are so various.

Virgil, "Moretum," lines 101–106

Little did you know that the motto inscribed on the Great Seal
of the United States refers to an herb salad. In this intense little
poem, dubiously attributed to Virgil, a peasant spends hundreds
of lines preparing a breakfast *moretum* (salad) out of the garlic
and herbs he has gathered that morning. The poet lingers on the
grinding and mixing of ingredients, the blending of shades of
green and white, until at last, *e pluribus unus*—out of many, one.
(Virgil uses *unus* because "color" is masculine in Latin; we use
the neuter form *unum* because the United States has no gender.)

Many of the founding fathers were gentlemen farmers, but it
is not certain that they had Virgil's salad in mind when they
adopted the phrase (already familiar in Britain, where it was the
motto of magazines compiled by various hands). Thomas Jefferson is credited with having suggested "*E pluribus unum,*" which
was then integrated into the first prototype of the Great Seal in
1776. Other elements of this rendering—the depiction of Moses
dividing the Red Sea, for example—did not make the final cut
in 1782.

Jefferson also proposed depicting a father presenting a bundle
of rods to his son—a reference to Aesop's tale of the bundle of
sticks [*see* FASCIST]—which would reinforce the message of *E
pluribus unum:* strength in unity. It all makes perfect sense; the
only remaining question is: which states are the garlic bulbs?

Love Conquers All

"Our hardships cannot move him,
Whether we drink from icy Hebrus in the midst of frosts
And endure the Sithonian snows of a damp winter,
Or whether, when the dying bark is dry in the high elm,
We tend Ethiopian sheep under the star of Cancer.
Love conquers all; we too yield to Love."

Virgil, "Tenth Eclogue," lines 64–69

In this eclogue (shepherd's song) a spurned lover commiserates with the poetic shepherds of Arcadia. He realizes nothing will win back his lover, whether it be drinking from an icy stream in the dead of winter or herding his sheep to Ethiopia during the dog-days of summer [*see* DOG DAYS]. The god Love, or Cupid, is not impressed with our pitiful attempts to undo his conquests: as Virgil famously puts it, "Love conquers all."

The Latin version of Virgil's phrase was long familiar, and even today is recognizable to the overeducated. Those who have read Chaucer's *Canterbury Tales,* or at least the General Prologue, will recall that the delicate prioress Madam Eglentine, whose charity is so manifest in the way she pampers her little dogs, wears a small gold brooch inscribed with the phrase *Amor vincit omnia*—"Love conquers all." The prioress seems to think Virgil meant "Love conquers everybody," as indeed the second half of the line ("we too yield to love") implies. But Virgil also means that "Love conquers all our efforts to win back someone's love." (Today the phrase simply means "give up.") By adopting from mythology the personification of love as a god, Virgil implies that he is a capricious and willful force beyond human control, laughing at our attempts to meddle in his business.

A Snake in the Grass

Damoetas: May he who loves you, Pollio, come to share in your fame;
     Let honey flow, and the harsh bramble-bush yield balsum.
Menalcas: Let him, Maevius, that does not hate Bavius, love your songs,
     And let him also yoke foxes and milk the he-goats.
Damoetas: May you who gather flowers and strawberries from the ground,
     Flee, you children, from the cold snake hiding in the grass.

Virgil, "Third Eclogue," lines 88–93

As two rustic poets compete in verse, each boasts at first that he
is more beloved by other shepherds and shepherdesses. But,
ominously, each then claims that he is the more perturbed and
persecuted by love. Love is to the shepherd as a storm is to trees,
or heavy showers to the harvest.

Since Virgil's shepherds are versifiers too, they also mean that
love is potentially ruinous to poets, even if it is a great source of
material. Virgil's own career supplies examples. His patron
Pollio's love is genuine, and Virgil intends to flatter him here.
Bavius and Maevius, on the other hand, betrayed the poet's
friendship, attacking him in their biting satires. The innocent
children who stoop to gather the fruits and flowers of love and
poetry should thus beware the "snake in the grass"—the hidden malice poised to attack.

When Virgil appears in
Dante's *Inferno* (canto 8), he trots
out his old saying, but refers to
Fortune this time rather than to
love: "her wisdom is hidden like
a snake in the grass." The phrase
"snake in the bush" appears in
English by 1677, and the familiar "snake in the grass" by 1696.

Time Flies

But meanwhile time flies, flies without recall,
While we linger on details, in love with our theme.
Enough of the herds: a second part of my task remains,
To tend to the sheep and the shaggy she-goats.

Virgil, *Georgics*, Book 3, lines 284–287

A "georgic" is a poem narrated by a farmer, and the form is thus suited to the practical discussion Virgil undertakes here. After several hundred lines of insights on the breeding and diseases of livestock, the speaker catches himself, noticing how quickly time has passed while he was rapt by so fascinating a subject. "*Fugit irreparabile tempus*," he says—or, as it was later permuted, "*tempus fugit*": "time flies," without repair. Virgil probably repeats a common Latin phrase, but his version is the most famous, and in context is quite close to our idea that "time flies when you're having fun."

The first occurrences of "time flies" in English, however, refer to it as a universal fact, whether one is having fun or not. Chaucer's clerk, in *The Canterbury Tales*, complains that "though we sleep or wake, or roam or ride,/ Ay fleeth the time, it nill no man abide." And as George Crabbe said in his poem *Sir Eustace Grey* (1807), "Some twenty years, I think, are gone;/ (Time flies, I know not how, away)." We now take it for granted that time is a winged creature with little care for human wishes, and its steady flight proves the vanity of our trying to catch it.

HORACE

(65–8 B.C.)

At the age of twenty, Quintus Horatius Flaccus, a promising young scholar, slipped up. He joined the rebel Brutus's army as an officer and helped wage war on the forces of Marc Antony, only to face defeat at the battle of Philippi in 42 B.C. On his return to Rome, Horace found that his land had been confiscated, and he was forced to take a low-paying position as a minor state secretary.

Horace figured that, so long as he was suffering, he might as well be an artist, and so he began writing verse. This brought him to the attention Rome's poetic "big guns," and they introduced him into the literary circle whose patron was the legendarily open-handed Maecenas. Horace became a new man, not only respected for his poetry but also a convert to the imperial cause, now represented by Caesar Augustus.

Horace's poetry falls into a few basic groups: the lyrical *Odes*, the miscellaneous *Epodes*, a series of *Epistles*, and the rather mild *Satires*. Horace exerted his greatest influence through his last epistle, which was later called *Ars Poetica*, or "The Art of Poetry." This grab-bag of observations and precepts became the basis of certain "rules" forced on dramatic poets and on the public in the sixteenth through eighteenth centuries, even though Horace is not quite so dogmatic. He did insist on poetic consistency, unity, and polish, and advocated imitating the great Greek classics which embodied those values.

Horace, who was regarded as a model of urbanity, wit, and good taste, was a staple of grammar-school education in Rome and Europe from the first century on, but now is read only by students of literary criticism.

If You Cast Out Nature with a Fork, It Will Still Return

If it behooves us to live according to nature,
And seeking a site to build a house is our first task,
Then what place could be more splendid than the country? . . .
Even you, amid your varied columns, nurse a forest
And praise a house with a prospect on distant fields.
You may cast out nature with a pitchfork, yet it will always return,
And stealthily break through your stupid disdain, victorious.

Horace, Epistles, Book 1, epistle 10, lines 12–14, 22–25

It's no longer so common for wits to quote the punch line of this poetic epistle, but it still has a certain irresistible ring. And back in the days when schoolchildren dutifully read their Horace, this phrase was a veritable proverb—and remained one until at least the late nineteenth century. The dramatist John Lyly, for example, wittily described the irrepressibility of human nature this way: "Why, though your son's folly be thrust up with a pair of horns on a fork, yet being natural, it will have [its] course" (*Mother Bombie*, 1594).

Horace's point is that his urbane friend boasts too much of the joys of city life. If man-made environs are so preferable to the country, then why, asks the poet, do city dwellers supplement their grand columns with mere trees, and why is such a premium placed on views of the countryside? Partisans of the city may pretend to raise something better in the place of nature, but nature returns through the back door. These, of course, were the heady days when civic development was in its flush; over the years, we've learned better its limitations. No one would want to live in a New York City without Central Park, no matter how infrequently he or she frolics on its grassy meadows.

The Golden Mean

Whoever is content with the golden mean
Is safe from the squalor
Of a ruined home, and temperately avoids
A house that provokes envy.

Horace, *Odes*, Book 2, ode 10, lines 5–8

According to Diogenes Laertius, the favorite saying of the Greek philosopher Cleobulus (sixth century B.C.) was "Moderation is best." By way of the younger sage Chilon, Aristotle turned the idea into a command: "Nothing in excess" [*see* p. 102]. But literature would have to wait for Horace to coin the phrase "golden mean" (*aurea mediocritas*) to name the happy state of mediocrity. Specifically, Horace counsels avoiding both lazy squalor and ambitious showiness; as the tall pine takes the brunt of the wind, the man of manifest achievement invites dangerous attention. Such practical caution is a far cry from Cleobulus and Aristotle—who counseled moderation not because it is safe, but because it is healthy and virtuous. Nevertheless, Horace's coinage has become the retroactive name of the Greek idea.

Why "golden mean" and not "silver mean," Horace does not explain—but poets also used *aureus* as a superlative meaning "excellent" or "beautiful." The adjective was adopted by English speakers without question, beginning with William Baldwin, who wrote in a 1587 work about the fall of ambitious princes that "The golden mean is best." Alexander Pope later imported the phrase into his translation of Homer's *Odyssey*, where the original has something like "In all things balance is better." Cleobulus may get the credit for turning the idea into a philosophical dictum, but it was already a poetic cliché.

Harmony in Discord

Even while you have such a contagious itch for profit,
You think upon nothing mean and still attend to the sublime:
. . . what covers the moon in darkness, what reveals it,
What is the design and what the power of the discordant harmony,
Whether Empedocles or Stertinius raves.

Horace, Epistles, Book 1, epistle 12, lines 14–15, 18–20

Though "harmony in discord" sounds more familiar to our ears, the phrase Horace coins is *concordia discors*, "discordant harmony"—but there's little difference in meaning. Whichever you prefer, Horace refers here to the philosophy of Empedocles, a wealthy Sicilian of the early fifth century B.C. Empedocles, after discovering air (empty space had earlier been thought simply empty), theorized that all things are composed of only four elements: earth, air, fire, and water. All change is caused by the union and disjunction of these elements; what unites them is love, what disjoins them is discord. Love and discord, forever at work, yield a universe that is both unified and constantly shifting—a harmonious discord, or discordant harmony. (New Age translation: it's a kind of yin-yang thing.)

Horace's face is not entirely straight here. He's writing to a friend who brags of philosophical sophistication while loudly complaining that he isn't well enough off. Horace pretends to be amazed that his friend, who's tending an estate he doesn't own, has so much time to ponder the mysteries of the universe—such as the causes of tides and discordant harmonies.

As for Empedocles, it appears that the harmonious universe was too discordant for him. By some accounts, including Matthew Arnold's in *Empedocles on Etna*, he ended his life by jumping into the Sicilian volcano. Maybe he had decided that fire made for a better end than earth, air, or water.

Purple Passages

Generally, weighty beginnings and great promises
Have one or another purple patch sewn in
To shine far and wide, as when Diana's sacred grove,
And the circuit of hastening waters through pleasant fields,
Or the River Rhine, or the rainbow is described.
But this is not their place.

> Horace, *Ars Poetica*, lines 14–18

Horace did the color purple no big favor by coining the phrase *purpureus pannus*, "purple patch." In his view, gaudy decorations on boasting verses only prove that the rumbling mountain has brought forth a ridiculous mouse [*see* p. 206]. Ornate and fanciful poetic metaphors are rarely appropriate and almost always badly handled. Horace would have the poet, especially the amateur, pursue the more modest aim of consistency.

The Latin *purpureus*, originally connoting "regal" since it described the color of kingly robes, insinuates that the bombastic poet thinks he's in the company of poetic royalty. Amusingly enough, Horace's art of poetry was first translated into English by Queen Elizabeth herself and published in 1598. She rendered *purpureus pannus* as "purple piece," which was later echoed in Horace-idolator Ben Jonson's version: "scarlet piece." (Horace appears in the flesh, as the author's stand-in, in Jonson's play *Poetaster.*) "Purple passages," now (along with "purple prose") the standard form of the phrase, does not seem to have appeared before the late nineteenth century, when a reviewer in the July 1895 issue of *The Century Illustrated Monthly Magazine* described the obviously superfluous embellishment of a piece of music: the performer "emphasiz[ed] the purpler passages with lifted voice and gesticulating finger."

Seize the Day

Be wise, strain your wine, and in this brief space
Cut back long hopes. Even as we speak, envious time
Flees: seize the day, trust little in tomorrow.

Horace, Odes, Book I, ode 11, lines 6–8

"Seize the day" (*carpe diem*) is now such a rousing cry that the reader is likely to be a little disappointed by Horace's original. The poet counsels his friend, not to run out and conquer the world, but to get back to work. No one knows what the gods have in store for him, Horace asserts; so the best thing is to stop dreaming about the future, admit that life is brief, and harvest today's crop.

This is one phrase I prefer to take out of context, thank you. Later interpretations of Horace's theme are much more romantic, or at least more interesting. Take, for example, Andrew Marvell's famous first lines of "To His Coy Mistress," which play on Horace's idea without directly quoting it. "Had we but world enough and time," the poem begins, "This coyness, Lady, were no crime." Marvell does not have his grape crop in mind. Life is short, but youth and beauty are even shorter, so "let us sport us while we may." Even while we now quote "seize the day" as a counsel against procrastination, it has about it an air of ambition, even idealism, and ambition is exactly what Horace is warning against.

PLINY THE ELDER

(A.D. 24–79)

Gaius Plinius Secundus, known as "Pliny the Elder" (uncle of Pliny the Younger), was born at Comum, now Como, in northern Italy. He was educated at Rome and then followed in his father's hoofsteps by joining the Roman cavalry. His career as an officer was quite distinguished, and it won him the regard of several emperors, Vespasian in particular [see MONEY DOESN'T SMELL]. He thus earned himself a number of important government posts, which allowed him to travel the breadth of the vast Roman empire.

Though an active man, Pliny was also dedicated to literary pursuits, and kept hundreds of notebooks full of details culled from Greek and Latin philosophers, scientists, and poets. Out of these he cobbled together his most famous, and only surviving, work, the *Naturalis Historia* [*Natural History*]. Basically a vast encyclopedia in thirty-seven books, its major topics are the physical universe, geography, ethnology, anthropology, physiology, zoology, botany, pharmacology, mineralogy and metallurgy. But the *Natural History* is less a work of science than a collection of anecdotes, popular errors, legends, remedies, and marvelous observations on everyday life in the Roman Empire.

Mixed in with material drawn from ancient "authorities" are many of Pliny's direct observations. In A.D. 79, his research took him to Mount Vesuvius, where he hoped to study volcanic activity at close range. Though he used a pillow to protect his head against the hail of ash and stones, Pliny finally succumbed to the sulphurous fumes and died of suffocation.

Canary

Juba reports that one of the Fortunate Isles is called Canaria after the multitude of huge canines who live there (two of which were brought back to him); the ruins of buildings are visible there; and while there is an abundance of fruits and birds of all species, date-bearing palms and pine trees also abound; there is also a copious supply of honey, papyrus too, and sheat-fish spawning in the streams; they are infested by beasts which are constantly cast up, rotting.

Pliny the Elder, *Natural History,*
Book 6, chapter 37

Why is a bird named after a dog? The little yellow songbirds we call canaries have little green ancestors who once lived on what are now Spain's Canary Islands. You might think that the islands are named after the birds, but according to Pliny such is not the case. "Canary" derives rather from the Latin word *canis,* "dog," and the name *Canaria* was given to one of these islands because of its population of fearsomely huge canines. Both the dogs and the birds were brought back to the Continent, but while the latter prospered, the former have since become extinct. The name *Canaria,* however, stuck to both the islands and the birds.

We owe the name to King Juba II of Mauretania, a friend of Caesar Augustus. Juba sent out expeditions to explore the African coast and its proximate islands, and it was one of these expeditions that happened upon the Canary Islands, which were supposed at the time to be the legendary "Fortunate Isles." The Greeks believed that the gods sent virtuous souls and particularly blessed mortals to these Isles as a sort of super retirement home.

Dog Days

Who does not know that the solar fires are excited at the rising of the dog-star, whose effect is great and is felt on earth? . . . Undoubtedly, dogs are most likely to be rabid during the whole of this time.

Pliny the Elder, *Natural History*, Book 2, chapter 40

Few things endure the ravages of time, but the days of August have always been dog days. Pliny explains the metaphor by pointing at the pitiful frenzy of canines in the late-summer heat, but references to this "fact" postdate the Greek expression *hemerai kynades*, "dog days." Originally, the Greeks dated their dog days according to the rising of the star Seirios, or Sirius, which means "burning." (Sirius now rises on August 11 at the latitude of Greenwich, but this is later than in ancient times.) Sirius also became known as the "dog star" when it was mythologized as the hunting-hound of the giant Orion, who lent his own name to a proximate star. It seems that Sirius earned this unflattering epithet because Orion's ferocious dog was the Greeks' best analogy for the way they felt dogged by the late-summer heat.

The Romans, adapting this mythology wholesale, called Sirius *Canicula*, "small dog," and translated the Greek *hemerai kynades* as *dies caniculares*, "days of the little dog." From the Latin derived the term "canicular days," which appears by the late fourteenth century in English. The less pedantic "dog days" does not appear until about the 1530s, when Sir Thomas Elyot explained that *Canicula* was the star "whereof canicular or dog days be named."

If Your Ears Burn, Someone Is Talking about You

Why do we believe the odd numbers are more vigorous in all things, which is shown in our observation of the days of a fever? . . . Why do we wish health to someone who sneezes—which even Tiberius Caesar, who everyone knows was very melancholy, enforced in carriages, so the report goes—and some think to religiously add the sneezer's name? And indeed it is believed that absent people divine, by the ringing in their ears, that people are talking about them.

Pliny the Elder, *Natural History*, Book 28, chapter 5

If you're going to write a book about everything in the world—which is basically what Pliny set out to do—sooner or later you'll get around to superstitions. Pliny arrives at this topic (merely one of about 20,000) in Book 28 of his *Natural History*, and his list of irrational habits mixes those that have endured (wishing someone "Happy New Year!", for example) with those that have gone the way of the chariot (e.g., belief in the power of odd numbers). Somewhere in between is the superstition that if your ears tingle (or glow, or burn), then someone is talking about you.

Chaucer provides the first surviving English reference to this fancy, in his *Troilus and Criseyde* (ca. 1374). Speaking of what he and Troilus will do after Cressida rides by their window, her uncle Pandarus jokes that "we shall speak of thee somewhat, I trow,/ Whan thou art gone, to doon [make] thy ears glow!" I guess he doesn't realize that he's missed the whole point by telling her in advance. In any case, the superstition later became a jest between confidants: "His ears must be burning" says the gossiper to the gossipee.

In a Nutshell

There are examples of sharpness of vision that are quite incredible. Cicero reports that there was a copy of Homer's *Iliad* inscribed on a piece of parchment enclosed in a nutshell. He also says there was a man who could see 135,000 paces [about 123 miles].

Pliny the Elder, *Natural History*, Book 7, chapter 21

Pliny usually reports the most incredible "facts" (like the story of Athanatus, who crossed a stage wearing 1,000 pounds of lead clothing) with barely a qualification, but in this case even he is given pause. Homer's *Iliad* is a poem of 15,690 lines in 24 books; even if there were someone who could read writing small enough to get the whole thing onto so tiny a parchment, one must doubt anyone's capacity to have inscribed it in the first place. Or perhaps that was one mighty big nut. (On the other hand, the Guinness Museum of World Records in San Francisco displays today a copy of the Lord's Prayer no bigger than the head of a nail; the nearby Ripley's Believe It or Not! Museum presents the prayer on a grain of rice.)

Pliny gains no real credibility by citing Cicero's report, since he or his source might have fabricated both the story and the citation. Nonetheless, this legendary *Iliad* became, if it wasn't already, the stuff of a Latin proverb: *"in nuce Ilias"*—"the *Iliad* in a nutshell." The phrase appears in English by 1579, when the polemicist Stephen Gosson alluded to "the whole world . . . drawn in a map; Homer's *Iliad* in a nutshell."

Though Shakespeare's Hamlet claims he could be "bounded in a nutshell" and rule that kingdom happily, "in a nutshell" as we use it didn't become a stand-alone phrase until the nineteenth century, when it was employed by writers such as Thomas Love Peacock, Charles Dickens, William Thackeray, and Robert Browning.

To Take with a Grain of Salt

> In the chambers of the great king Mithridates, Cneius Pompeius discovered in a private notebook, in the king's own hand, the formula for an antidote: two dry nuts, the same number of figs, and twenty leaves of rue ground together, with a grain of salt added; whoever took this on an empty stomach would be harmed by no poison that day.
>
> Pliny the Elder, *Natural History*, Book 23, chapter 77

If you've ever wondered what a "mithridate" is, look no further: Pliny supplies the recipe. According to legend, King Mithridates VI of Pontus (now in Turkey), who died circa 63 B.C., came up with a fool-proof concoction that was not only an antidote to any poison, but also a preventative. (It didn't immunize him, however, against the sword of one of his own guards.) Early pharmacologists named this mixture after the king, taking it on faith that the thing actually worked. Later, when the original recipe proved a bust—which was around the seventeenth century—the word "mithridate" was applied to any other brand of snake-oil assumed to be a universal antidote.

But this is all by the way of arriving at the recipe's famous last words: "with the addition of a grain of salt." Pliny's phrasing is generally agreed to be the source of the relatively late Latin expression *cum grano salis*, "with a grain of salt"—meaning "with a certain reservation of belief."

Pliny brings all this up not to illustrate the power of salt, but rather the potency of the walnut, to which he devotes an entire chapter. Among the nut's powers are to induce headaches and vomiting if eaten dry, to mollify onions, to cure ear inflammations, to heal dog bites, to promote the growth of a baby's hair when burned and mixed with wine, to expel tapeworms, and to cure rabies. But only if taken with a grain of salt.

JUVENAL

(ca. A.D. 60–128)

"Juvenal" isn't the proper name of Decimus Junius Juvenalis, but rather his cognomen or nickname, derived from the Latin for "juvenile" or "youthful." Unfortunately, nothing is known of his youth and not much more about the rest of his life, apart from what we may infer from his own writings.

Juvenal's extant work comprises sixteen satiric poems, the last fragmentary, which detail the decline and corruption of the Roman Empire in the early second century A.D. These satires would become famous for their bitterness and moral exasperation, though at the time they seem to have been paid little attention, since they did absolutely no good. Even Juvenal himself despaired of improving Roman morals; his attacks on depravity, hypocrisy, cruelty, and ingratitude seem expressions of frustration more than exhortations to reform.

The earliest of these satires lends some credence to later stories that Juvenal's outspoken criticisms gave offense to the emperor Domitian, who ruled from A.D. 81 to 96. According to the legends, Juvenal was exiled until the emperor's death, when he returned to Rome a pauper. His published satires show that he was subsequently squeamish of offending powerful contemporaries, so his attacks are directed at past generations. Their application to the present, however, must have been pretty obvious.

His rough and bitterly ironic style is in marked contrast to the milder tones of Horace's satires, and struck later writers as much more effective. Juvenal had an enormous influence on English satire from Chaucer to Swift and beyond.

Bread and Circuses

Long since, because we can sell our votes to no one,
We have thrown off our cares; those who once bestowed
Rule, the *fasces*, legions, everything, now refrain,
And hunger for only two things:
Bread and circuses.

Juvenal, "Tenth Satire," lines 78–82

While Juvenal's usual modus operandi is to rake his contemporaries over the coals by pretending to condemn the faults of ancestors, in this satire he comes right out and points the finger at present-day apathy and cynicism. Since its applause has lost its power over men of ambition, the public has stopped taking its civic responsibilities seriously. Power has turned into a vicious, competitive game that aspiring men play, and the people just sit back and watch them rise and fall, still applauding today's victor and booing today's victim, but now in vain. Society has become amoral and irrational, and the people cowardly and lazy; all they ask for is "bread and circuses": a full belly and interesting shows.

"Bread and circuses" still refers to keeping a population's mind off the quality of its government by providing it with sufficient food and enough trivial distractions. So long as the citizen is well-fed and stimulated, he or she will settle for whoever is in power. Yet circuses alone sometimes suffice when provision is hard to come by, as the *Times* of London observed in the depression year of 1930: "Processions are good things, and there is never a better time for the circuses than when the bread is dear or scarce."

Who Shall Guard the Guardians?

"Who are you kidding? Stage this farce for someone else! A guarantee:
I contend you are fully a man. So I contend; will you confess?
Or shall I torture the truth out of the servant girls?" I'm aware
Of the advice and warnings of all my old friends:
"Confine them behind a bolted door." But who shall guard
The guardians, who now, for a fitting reward, hush up
The deceits of these lewd girls? They conspire in silence:
Your prudent wife provides for this, and she starts with your guards.

Juvenal, "Sixth Satire," lines O 27–34

In this antifeminist satire, Juvenal takes up the question of how
a man may prevent his wife's infidelity. As far as he sees it, any
effort is doomed. Here he addresses the practice of employing
a eunuch to guard one's woman; he's willing to bet that the
supposed eunuch is "completely a man," in other words, an
impostor. (Such an imposture had been the subject of one of
Terence's most famous plays: *The Eunuch*.) You can put your wife
under guard, says the satirist, but "who shall guard the guardians?"

I'm willing to bet that those who intone this famous phrase
today haven't read their Juvenal. "Who shall guard the guardians" is now uttered in the spirit of high-minded civic conscien-
tiousness, with a finger pointed at some corrupt official. Juvenal's
line, presented in deadpan Latin, is the epigraph of the 1987
Tower Commission Report, in which a presidential review board
gives account of the Iran–Contra scandal. It's a pretty large step
from trying to lock up one's wife to trying to keep the executive
branch from selling TOW missiles to Iran.

A Rare Bird

"Is there no one among these crowds who seems deserving to you?"
Let her be beautiful, becoming, rich, and fertile; let her place
Ancient ancestors in her galleries; let her be more chaste
Than all the Sabine women, with disheveled hair, who broke off the war:
A rare bird, as rare on earth as a black swan;
Who could bear a wife so possessed of all things?

Juvenal, "Sixth Satire," lines 161–166

Juvenal's satires don't reveal a very high opinion of women, who are depicted as lustful, greedy, power-hungry, and vain. When an anonymous voice asks whether there isn't one woman he would consider marrying, the narrator of the "Sixth Satire" details the prerequisites. She must be modest, attractive, rich, able to bear children, reverent of her ancestors, and more virginal than the Sabine women before they were raped [*see* THE SABINE WOMEN]. A woman like this, according to the narrator, would be a "rare bird" (*rara avis*) indeed. But of course, the rare creature is also a misfit; the rarest swan is a black one. So be it, says the narrator; who could stand a wife who was perfect?

Black swans were later discovered in Australia, but that didn't put Juvenal's phrase out of commission. The phrase "rare bird" has been adopted out of its satirical and misogynistic context to refer to an extraordinary individual of either sex or any color.

A Sound Mind in a Sound Body

You should pray for a sound mind in a sound body;
Beg for a bold spirit free from the fear of death,
Which reckons length of life the least among the gifts
Of nature; which can bear any burden whatsoever;
Which knows not anger, desires nothing, and thinks
The trials and harsh labors of Hercules preferable
To the loves and banquets and cushions of Sardanapalus.

Juvenal, "Tenth Satire," lines 356–362

"A sound mind in a sound body" (*mens sana in corpore sano*) is about all this narrator thinks it's worth praying for, since if we pray for other supposed benefits—children, for example—who knows what the gods will send us? (Perhaps the sort of children we've got to ship out to prep schools for sounder minds and sounder bodies.)

Classical thinkers tended to segregate mind (or spirit) from body (or matter); but on the other hand they believed that the health and discipline of the flesh in fact promoted a healthy mind, and vice versa. In other words, "sound of body, sound of mind," a maxim derived from but not identical to Juvenal's. Where we use the phrase to mean "do your push-ups every night and you'll think more clearly in the morning," Juvenal takes a sound body for granted and then asserts that we need sounder minds in order to put our healthy bodies to better use.

Juvenal's satire flirts with stoicism [*see* STOIC]. Hate and desire are afflictions that trouble the spirit, of course, but by doing so they lead the body into weakness, just as they originate in the flesh. The narrator of the poem exhorts us to play Hercules, stoutly enduring trials and tribulations, rather than falling prey to the luxuriance and lethargy of the notorious Assyrian king Sardanapalus.

Thumbs Up / Thumbs Down

These men once were horn-blowers and attendants
At every municipal arena, known as trumpeters in every village.
Now they present their own spectacles, and, to win applause,
Kill whomever the mob gives the "thumbs up." Then they go back
To contracting for public toilets, and why not anything else,
Since they're the sort Fortune lifts up from baseness
To the greatest heights whenever she wants a laugh?

Juvenal, "Third Satire," lines 34–40

Juvenal refers to the Roman custom of spectators' voting on the fate of wounded gladiators with their thumbs. You might think a gladiator would appreciate the crowd's "thumbs up" (*verso pollice*), but exactly the opposite is true. Where we give thumbs up as a sign of approval, it meant death to its Roman recipient—much to the crowd's delight. Thumbs down, signifying "swords down," meant the loser was worth more to them alive than dead, and he was spared to make up for his disgrace the next time out. Keep this in mind next time you give somebody the "thumbs up."

Our topsy-turvy interpretation of this custom seems to be the work of the French artist Léon Gérôme. Gérôme understood the Latin *verso* ("turned") to mean "turned down," and thus in his painting *Pollice Verso* (1873) he represents the death sentence with the thumbs-down gesture. The painting proved so popular that Gérôme's mistake stuck, probably never to be unstuck again.

Gladiatorial shows have been traced back as far as 264 B.C., but their popularity grew markedly in the late days of the Roman republic and during the period of empire—that is, from about the first century B.C. onward. At first, these bloody contests were exclusive to funeral rites, but they later became a feature of all important public events and even of some private banquets.

Private men spent enormous sums staging these battles, despite the government's attempts to impose limits. Prisoners of war and slaves were sent to gladiatorial academies for training and then were rented out for parties.

The shows sponsored by the government and put on at public expense were initially held at the infamous Circus Maximus, Rome's principal stadium for chariot racing. Later, the gladiators were moved into large amphitheaters, and advertisements were posted that listed the combatants' names and trumpeted their past achievements. After a few *pro forma* spectacles, the gladiators got down to serious business. Whenever a combatant was seriously wounded, the presiding judge, or referee, was called upon to determine whether the man should live or die, depending on how well he had put up a fight. The judge usually deferred to the pleasure of the audience, who would cheer, applaud, and give the thumbs down if they liked the man, who was then carted off to lick his wounds. But if they gave him the silent thumbs-up treatment, his opponent was given the signal to finish him off. The corpse was then dragged off with a hook.

Roman History

If we follow the empire's early historians, Rome was founded in the eighth century B.C., but Roman history itself dates only from about the second century B.C., when Cato the Censor, wrote his *Origins* (of Italian cities) from about 170 to 150 B.C.

Of the writers I rely on in this section—comprising phrases derived from particular Roman people and events—the earliest is Titus Livius, or Livy (59 B.C.–A.D. 17). He began his *History of Rome* when he was thirty and worked on it until his death, leaving behind 142 books, thirty-five of which survive. Livy was not overly concerned to separate fact from fiction, so he begins his history with the wanderings of Aeneas, moves on to the founding of Rome by Romulus and Remus [*see* p. 164], and thereafter focuses on exemplary tales of the ideal Roman character. Livy turned to the past to avert his eyes from Rome's present miseries and corruptions; and in fact the purpose of his *History* is to draw an unflattering contrast between the greatness of the Romans' ancestors and the moral turpitude of his contemporaries.

Perhaps the greatest of all ancient historians is Publius Cornelius Tacitus (ca. A.D. 55–118), who made himself known in Rome first as an orator, later as a senator during the hair-raising reign of the emperor Domitian (A.D. 81–96), and finally as a consul. Like Livy's work, Tacitus's survives only in fragments; but we do have a good part of the *Annals* and of the *Histories*, which between them chronicle events from the reigns of Tiberius to Domitian. Tacitus is a brilliant observer with a keen wit and a penchant for epigrams; yet he claims to write "*sine ira et studio*"— without anger or partisanship. Indeed, he is less credulous than Livy, and he does his best to report impartially on emperors he clearly considered monsters.

Many of the best stories of Roman history are not to be found in histories, but rather in biographies. I rely here on the two classical biographers who survived longest in European letters: Plutarch and Suetonius. Plutarch (ca. A.D. 46–120), born in central Greece under Roman occupation, was an Academic philosopher [*see* p. 85] as well as a biographer, and we have encountered some of his ethical writings elsewhere [*see* EUREKA! *and* NATURE ABHORS A VACUUM]. Plutarch is best remembered for his *Parallel Lives*, which comprises forty-six paired biographies, each pair including the lives of one famous Greek and one famous Roman.

Plutarch, like Livy, is primarily concerned to illustrate his subjects' moral character; Gaius Suetonius Tranquillus (ca. A.D. 69–140), on the other hand, was more interested in compiling as many naked facts and legends about his subject as possible, even when they came from conflicting sources. Suetonius, who helped make historical writing more biographical, is most famous for his *Lives of the Caesars* from Julius to Domitian, published ca. A.D. 121. These *Lives* are perhaps more entertaining than accurate, but they record many legendary events that *ought* to be true even if they're not.

Romulus and Remus

I am sure the fates had already decided upon the founding of this great city and the inception of our imperial power, second only to the gods'. The Vestal Virgin was raped, and when she had given birth to twins, she named Mars as the father of her dubious offspring—whether because it was true or because it would appear more honorable if a god were author of the crime. But neither gods nor men defended either her or her children from the king's cruelty: he ordered the Vestal chained and put in custody, and the boys cast into a river.

Livy, *The History of Rome*, Book 1, chapter 4

Ever wondered why the symbol of Rome is two guys nursing on some sort of beast? Read on.

The early history of Rome, such as Livy tells it, was a rather bloody and fratricidal business. According to legend, the Trojan hero Aeneas—namesake of Virgil's epic *The Aeneid*—escaped the destruction of Troy and, guided by the gods, settled with his men in central Italy. After forcing the local Latins to submit, Aeneas became their king. Thirteen generations later, Proca reigned, and then named as his successor his elder son Numitor.

Proca's younger son Amulius, however, decided he wasn't having any of this and seized the crown. After killing all of Numitor's male children, Amulius threw his niece Rhea Silvia into a nunnery, more or less. By making her a Vestal Virgin—a priestess in the service of the hearth-goddess Vesta—he intended to assure that she would bear no children to rival his for the throne.

Well, Amulius's well-laid plans went seriously awry. Rhea Silvia one day found herself with twin sons, and her claim that Mars was the father didn't forestall Amulius's vindictive response. Rhea herself was tossed to the flames, and her sons condemned to be drowned. Amulius's servants botched the drowning part, and—still following me?—the twins were rescued by a she-wolf. From there, the boys—Romulus and Remus by name—were adopted by the king's herdsman, grew into bold and strong youths, and took to harassing local brigands.

By chance, Remus fell into the hands of Numitor, who eventually guessed the boy's identity. Plots were hatched, and Romulus, with his brother's help, murdered their great-uncle Amulius, restoring the crown to their grandfather. The boys' next project was to establish a settlement at the place where they were supposed to have been drowned. Unfortunately, even before the settlement was built the twins fell into an argument over who should govern it. One thing led to another, and Romulus, Cain-like, put his brother out of the picture for good. That over with, he bestowed his name on the new settlement, which ultimately grew into what Livy calls an empire "second only to the gods'," Rome.

The Seven Hills of Rome

When San Francisco, California, claims to be the "Rome of the West," its main—and perhaps only—claim to the comparison is that it is built, like Rome, on seven hills. (Actually, Rome has more than seven hills, but the smaller ones aren't counted.) We'll leave Californian topography to others to account for; in Rome's case, the hills were carved out by the now relatively placid Tiber River and its tributary streams, which had an easy job of it, given the pliant floor of the river basin. The ancient Romans bestowed a title on each of the hills, which are as follows:

THE CAPITOLINE was, according to Livy, consecrated by Romulus to the god Jupiter, and then became the site of Rome's first and greatest temple. As the highest of Rome's hills, it was named *capitolium,* from *caput* ("head, top, summit"). The Capitoline, as the citadel of Rome, is the source of our word "capitol."

THE PALATINE is the centermost hill, and is said by ancient historians to have been the first settled. Livy claims the hill was named after Pallanteum, an Italian settlement founded by Greeks from Arcadia. By the third century B.C., the Palatine had become a fashionable residential district. Its showy buildings, in particular Augustus Caesar's, were later called *palatia,* the source of our word "palace."

THE AVENTINE is where Romulus was supposed to have killed his brother Remus [*see* p. 165], and was therefore regarded by the Romans as a place of ill fortune. The authorities generously bestowed the hill upon the Roman people for settlement in 456 B.C. Livy reports that it was named after Aventius, thirteenth king of the Latins, who was buried there.

THE CAELIAN is, by unreliable report, named after Caelius Vibenna, a Tuscan who joined the Romans to fight back their enemies after the rape of the Sabine Women [*see* p. 168].

THE ESQUILINE is actually an eastern plateau, whose name derives, for obscure reasons, from *excolo,* "to cultivate." The emperor Augustus gave the whole thing to the wealthy patron Maecenas, who built a mansion there that he, in turn, bequeathed to Augustus.

THE VIMINAL is named after the osier tree, a species of willow, which grew there in number. In Latin the tree was called *vimen,* plural *vimines,* which lends the osier its modern scientific name, *salix viminalis.*

THE QUIRINAL, northernmost of the hills, derives its name from the Sabine town of Cures. After the conflict between the Romans and Sabines was resolved and the peoples were united [*see* THE SABINE WOMEN], the Romans as a friendly gesture took on the name "Quirites," after Cures. The hill was supposed to have been originally settled by the Sabines, and thus it adopted the new title as well. A traffic tunnel runs through it today.

The Sabine Women

> Many people gathered at Rome, for they were eager to see the new city. . . .
> Even the Sabines came, and brought their wives and children with them.
> . . . When the time had come for the spectacles, and the visitors' eyes and
> minds were all fixed upon them, then the Romans sprang their plot; upon a
> given signal, the Roman youths broke out to seize the virgins.
>
> Livy, *The History of Rome*, Book 1, chapter 9

Circa 750 B.C., the Romans, finding themselves short on women,
decide to throw a big party. They send out word that they'll be
celebrating Consualia—a festival in honor of Neptune—in a
grand style, and invite the countryside to join in. The neighbors
have viewed the new city with a mixture of fear, envy, and
curiosity—plus a measure of protective caution on the part of
local fathers with single daughters. But they let their curiosity
get the better of their fear and fall into the Romans' trap. While
everyone is gawking at the show, the hosts grab the girls and
spirit them off; as Livy drily puts it, "By this act of violence the
fun of the festival broke up in panic." The girls' parents make
a quick getaway, and the Romans promptly marry their prizes.

Now, these girls hailed from a number of settlements, but the
most powerful figure in the region was the king of the Sabines,
a local hill people; so all the aggrieved parties appealed to him
for justice. Because the Sabines took the leading role in aveng-
ing the Romans' outrage, this event has become known as the
rape of the Sabine women. According to Livy, everyone kisses
and makes up in the end, after the Sabine women intercede on
behalf of both their fathers and their husbands. Then Rome,
typically, absorbs the Sabine state. The whole affair is a fine
illustration of the character of early Rome, but that's about all it
is; modern historians have written it off as a fiction.

A Pyrrhic Victory

According to some accounts, when one of his men rejoiced at the victory they had won, Pyrrhus gave this answer: "If we win another of the price, we are utterly undone."

Plutarch, *Life of Pyrrhus*, chapter 21

The ambitious and unfortunate king Pyrrhus is now remembered only by this phrase, but in his own day he caused quite a stir. In 307 B.C., at the age of twelve, Pyrrhus took charge of the kingdom of Epirus established by Alexander the Great in what is today northwestern Greece and southern Albania. After a series of gains and setbacks against his former Macedonian mentors, Pyrrhus joined war with the Romans in 280 B.C. His most memorable battle occurred in 279 at the city of Asculum, now Ascoli Piceno, near the Adriatic coast.

Pyrrhus found himself in rather inconvenient terrain. For one thing, his cavalry couldn't effectively negotiate the surrounding hills, and for another he faced his enemy across a swift river banked with woods, which impeded his charge of elephants. Pyrrhus lost a good number of men. When the battle moved to level ground, the Romans were so terrified of being stomped on by the enemy's pachyderms that they fought all the more savagely, inflicting severe losses on the Epirians. Nevertheless, the Romans were finally forced to retreat, but only after the two sides had suffered a combined loss of 15,000 men, including most of the Epirian generals. It was then that Pyrrhus is said to have made his famous remark that another such victory would be his ruin—the source of our phrase "Pyrrhic victory," apparently coined by the British newspaper *The Daily Telegraph* in 1885.

Caesar

However "Caesar" became the nickname of Gaius Julius—whom we know as "Julius Caesar" [*see* CAESAREAN SECTION]—it later became the property of the first five Roman emperors, from Augustus to Nero, for whom the reference to Julius provided both historical continuity and imperial legitimacy. Thereafter, "Caesar" stopped being a name and became an honorific, the equivalent of "emperor." In later usage, "caesar" was the title given to the heir presumptive to the empire.

It appears that "caesar" (pronounced "kai-sar") was the first Latin word to be adopted into the Teutonic language, whence it passed in various forms into Gothic, Frisian, German, Dutch, English, and Norse (Icelandic). The Gothic form was "kaisar," which yielded the German and Middle English form "kaiser"—later a term applied to German rulers of the Holy Roman Empire, but only by foreigners. (The term was then passed on to Austrian emperors from 1804–1918, and to Germans from 1871–1918.) On another front, Old Slavonic adopted its own version of "caesar," which was handed on to Russian in the form "tsar"—later misspelled "czar" in a 1549 treatise that was the primary Western source of information on things Russian.

Gaius Julius also lent his name to the Spanish city Caesaris, later Xeres and now Jerez de la Frontera. Englishmen corrupted the name "Xeres" into "sherris," whence the name "sherry" for the still wine produced near the city. But that other Caesar in a bottle, the Caesar salad dressing, is not named after Julius but, like the salad itself, after Caesar Cardini, who introduced the dish in 1924 at his Tijuana restaurant. (In some versions of the story, it was actually Caesar's brother Alex who devised the recipe.) Anchovies were no part of the original dish, but were added later over Cardini's protests.

A Caesarean Section

As for the term "Caesares," the Romans usually gave that name to children born either by tearing their mother's womb [*caeso matris utero*], or with a bush of hair growing on their heads [*cum caesarie*], or else grey-eyed [*oculis caesiis*].

Philemon Holland, Supplement (1606) to Suetonius, *The Deified Julius*

What we have here is a rather complicated chicken and egg problem. The egg in this case is the name Caesar, which many people believe was bestowed on Julius because he was born by what we now call "Caesarean section"—the Latin *caeso matris utero* meaning "torn from the mother's womb."

Yet Suetonius's first translator, Philemon Holland, reports that "Caesar" had been the surname of a Roman family and later the nickname of various members of the Julian clan, including Gaius Julius Caesar. (Julius Caesar's first name isn't Julius, but Gaius, and his surname isn't Caesar, but Julius.) He then asserts that the Julii had no special claim to the nickname, since it was also bestowed on babies born in a peculiar manner, for example through a cut womb. An infant with gray or "cutting eyes" (*ocules caesis*) might also lay claim to the name Caesar, as might a hairy one, since the Latin for "hair" is *caesaries*.

Is it mere coincidence that Julius Caesar was born—as his early biographers reported—by Caesarean section, or is this a fable based on the family nickname? Probably the latter, since the Romans generally limited Caesarean sections to those cases in which the mother died before delivery, and Caesar's mother survived his birth. Yet the English word "Caesarean" derives from the person Caesar rather than from the Latin word *caesum*, and was first used to mean "an adherent of the emperor." The term "Caesarean section," apparently based on the dubious tale of Caesar's birth, appeared about ninety years later.

To Cross the Rubicon

Now when Caesar had overtaken his cohorts at the river Rubicon, which was the utmost boundary of his province, he rested for a while; then, considering how great an enterprise he was undertaking, turned to those who stood next to him and said, "As yet, friends, we are able to turn back; but once we pass over this little bridge, there will be no business but by force of arms and dint of sword."

Suetonius, *The Deified Julius*, paragraph 31

For such a small river, the Rubicon has a mighty reputation. The Rubicon, or Rubico, which joined the Adriatic Sea near present-day Rimini in Italy, played a substantial role in the history of the Roman Empire in 49 B.C. This little stream divided Italy proper from the Roman province of Cisalpine Gaul, and thus divided territory controlled by Pompey, who held power at the center, from territory controlled by Julius Caesar, who held power in Gaul and Illyricum (in the Balkans).

As Suetonius tells the tale, the authorities in Rome have been growing increasingly nervous about Caesar's army, which had lately scored numerous successes in expanding and consolidating the empire. Around 51 B.C., in a time of peace, one of the Roman consuls proposed that Caesar's now unnecessary army be disbanded and that Caesar himself be demoted from his powerful post as proconsul—that is, as governor of his provinces. But Caesar realized that he was the "leading man of the state," as Suetonius puts it, and would not brook humiliation. After suffering further indignities, Caesar masses an army on the near bank of the Rubicon, and after slight hesitation casts his die and decides to cross [*see* THE DIE IS CAST].

By crossing the Rubicon, Caesar initiates civil war. This famous act, as enshrined in our catch-phrase "to cross the Rubicon," came to stand for making a momentous decision, if one short of declaring war, from which there is no turning back. The metaphor appeared in English by the early seventeenth century, sometimes in the form "to pass the Rubicon." As one character says in John Crowne's play *The English Friar* (1690), "I'll be hanged if this fellow got [begot] me. Some Caesar pass'd my mother's Rubicon; would I had his commentaries"—a witty reference to Caesar's *Commentaries* on the Gallic War. Charlotte Brontë has Jane Eyre use the figure, when she marks "A pause— in which I began to steady the palsy of my nerves, and to feel that the rubicon was passed" (*Jane Eyre*, 1847).

"Rubicon" appears as a verb in the late nineteenth century, when by some logic it came to refer to a decisive victory at cribbage. R. F. Foster, in his 1897 edition of *The Complete Hoyle*, produces this mellifluous definition: "Rubiconed, lurched, defeated before getting half way."

If you were wondering whether the Rubicon is still there, that's something the Italians haven't quite figured out. No fewer than three rivers have laid claim to identity with the ancient landmark, but each claim is pretty dubious. The three are the Pisciatello, the Fiumicino, and the Uso; at present, the Fiumicino, which lies between the other two, has been officially dubbed the "Rubicone."

The Die Is Cast

As he stood still and full of doubt, he happened to see something very strange. All of a sudden there appeared to him a certain man of extraordinary stature and shape, sitting close by and piping on a reed. Now when, besides the shepherds and herdsmen, many soldiers rushed over to hear him, among them the trumpeters, he snatched from one a trumpet, leapt forth to the river, and, beginning with a mighty blast to sound the battle, forged ahead to the other bank. Caesar then spoke: "Let us march on, and go wherever the tokens of the gods and the provocations of our enemies call us. The die is cast."

Suetonius, *The Deified Julius*, paragraph 32

In early 49 B.C., Julius Caesar assembles his army at the bank of the river Rubicon, but hesitates to cross [*see* p. 172]. The historian Suetonius relates what happens next. A god-like figure appears on the bank, pipes on a reed, grabs someone's trumpet, renders a flourish, and shows the astonished Caesar the way over the river. Suetonius presents this event as a fact; what that says about the credibility of the rest of his report, I leave to the reader to determine. In any case, Caesar, according to the historian, draws the obvious conclusion from this sign, and announces that "The die is cast." Civil war ensues.

What Caesar means is that by forging the Rubicon he will pass a point of no return, and fate will decide the outcome. Perhaps he should have said "the coin is flipped," since that would offer clear-cut win/loss options; what happens if the die comes up showing a four is hard to imagine. Since Roman dice, like ours, had six sides, there are many more ways to lose than to win. Flipping a coin would be too easy for Caesar; yet if the gods have loaded the die, he can still be pretty certain of the outcome. It just *looks* a lot harder. He wins the war, of course.

Several people have asked me whether Caesar might actually mean by "the die is cast" that "the metal template has been molded." An interesting possibility, but only possible in English. Caesar's word for "die" is *alea,* one of a pair of dice—and the root of our word "aleatory" ("depending on chance"). The first English translation, by Philemon Holland in 1606, in fact reads "the die be thrown," which makes the matter clearer. Though Caesar *might* have meant that the course of future events would be stamped out with a metal die, he could hardly have been contemplating throwing one over the Rubicon.

I Came, I Saw, I Conquered

Having finished all his wars, Caesar rode in five triumphs: four times in the same month, with a few days between each triumph, after vanquishing Scipio; and once again after he had overcome the children of Pompey. . . . In his Pontic triumph, amidst the pageants and pomp, he caused to be carried before him an inscription of these three words: *Veni vidi, vici;* and this signified, not the outcome of the war, which other conquerors would have celebrated, but rather his speed in dispatching the war.

Suetonius, *The Deified Julius*, paragraph 37

After crossing the Rubicon [*see* p. 172], Julius Caesar crushes his opposition within about four years. Particularly efficient was his rout of Pompey's forces at Pontus, in northeast Asia Minor. Some versions of the story, such as Plutarch's, have Caesar immediately sending word to Rome that *"Veni, vidi, vici"*—"I came, I saw, I conquered"—a magnificent brag that mirrors the brevity of the campaign in economy of expression.

In Suetonius's version, however, which was published after Plutarch's, Caesar waits until after the wars are over and inscribes the phrase for display in a victory procession. Suetonius's Caesar is not so impressive, as he shows more calculation in self-aggrandizement; but whenever Caesar composed his famous phrase, it has captured everyone's imagination ever since. Of course, nobody uses *"Veni, vidi, vici"* today unless ironically. Shakespeare's Sir John Falstaff set the pace when, bragging of a rare triumph, he jokes that he "may justly say, with the hook-nosed fellow of Rome, 'I came, saw, and overcame'" (*Henry the Fourth, Part 2*, Act 4, scene 3).

Beware the Ides of March

There was a certain soothsayer that had long before given Caesar warning to take heed of the Ides of March (which is the fifteenth of the month), for on that day he should be in great danger. The day having arrived, Caesar went to the Senate-house and spoke merrily to the soothsayer, saying: "The Ides of March is come." "So it is," the soothsayer answered softly, "but yet it is not past."

Plutarch, *Life of Julius Caesar*

While many readers will associate "Beware the Ides of March" with Shakespeare's *Julius Caesar*, in fact the Bard based the events of that play on Plutarch's *Life of Julius Caesar*, one of a series of lives written by the Greek biographer and philosopher (d. ca. A.D. 120) and translated into English by Sir Thomas North in 1579. (I have adapted North's translation here.)

Unbeknownst to Caesar, there is a conspiracy to dispatch him, spearheaded by Gaius Cassius and Marcus Brutus, two men Caesar refers to as "pale-visaged and carrion lean people." (In Shakespeare, Cassius has "a lean and hungry look.") Caesar detects their discontent, but he refuses to acknowledge any threat. Caesar also ignores a multitude of other strange signs of impending disaster—including the soothsayer's warning—because he thinks the best death is "Death unlooked for." This is the death that finds him on the Ides of March.

In the Julian calendar, instituted by Caesar himself [*see* p. 189], the Ides varies with the month. The Ides of March, May, July, and October is the fifteenth; the Ides of the remaining months falls on the thirteenth. In Caesar's time, the Ides was calibrated to the full moon.

Et Tu, Brute?

When they saw that Caesar had settled in his place, the conspirators stood around him as if to do him honor, and immediately Tullius Cimber, who had taken the lead, stepped closer as if to make some request. When Caesar seemed to take offense, and with a gesture put him off until another time, Cimber caught hold of his toga at both shoulders. At this Caesar cried out, "This is violence!", whereupon one of the two Cascas attacked him frontally, wounding him a little beneath the throat. . . . And so he was stabbed with three and twenty wounds, having uttered no word save one groan upon the first thrust; some have written, however, that as Marcus Brutus came running upon him, he cried in Greek, *kai su, teknon*, "And thou, my son?"

Suetonius, *The Deified Julius*, paragraph 82

By 44 B.C. Julius Caesar had become unpopular in several quarters, and on the Ides of March in that year he fell victim to an assassination plot [*see* BEWARE THE IDES OF MARCH]. Among those who planted their blades in the dictator was Marcus Brutus, whom Caesar apparently considered almost as a son. Suetonius reports, but cannot confirm, the assertion of earlier writers (whose works are lost) that Caesar uttered his famous reproach of Brutus in Greek—in other words, if he said anything to Brutus, he did not say "And you too, Brutus?", nor did he say it in Latin, in which language the supposed utterance has become famous: "*Et tu, Brute?*" (In the earlier account by Plutarch, Caesar says nothing, but only pulls his gown over his head.)

The Latin phrase doesn't appear in English until the late sixteenth century. Shakespeare uses it in *Julius Caesar* (1599; Act 3, scene 1), cleverly having Caesar switch from English to Latin just as legend had Caesar switching from Latin to Greek. But "*Et tu, Brute*" had already appeared in *The True Tragedy of Richard Duke of York* (published 1595), which is believed to be an unreliable reconstruction of Shakespeare's own *Henry the Sixth, Part 3* (1590–1591).

Make Haste Slowly

Augustus considered nothing less becoming an accomplished leader than haste and temerity. Thus he often would utter such phrases as "More haste, less speed"; "A wary captain is better than a bold"; and "Soon enough is that done which is well done."

Suetonius, *The Deified Augustus*, paragraph 25

Though Caesar Augustus, the adopted heir of Julius Caesar, was no stranger to cruelty and war, he has traditionally been regarded as an imposer of peace on a Roman empire torn by civil war. After defeating his rival Marc Antony in 31 B.C., he became the *de facto* emperor, though he made show of reviving the republic and returning power to the people. Augustus was never uncomfortable enough with his imperial power to surrender it, but he was also a traditionalist concerned to preserve the old Roman values and fond of proverbial sayings.

Suetonius records some of the emperor's favorite cautionary proverbs; the second is borrowed from Euripides and the third from Cato the Censor. The most famous is the first, which the historian quotes in Greek but whose origin has not been traced. The Latin version is *festina lente*: "make haste slowly." This paradoxical saying is equivalent to Chaucer's aphorism in *Troilus and Criseyde* (ca. 1374): "He hasteth well that wisely can abide"— that is, a speedy success rests on knowing how to bide one's time and wait for the opportune moment.

The Latin saying itself (which Augustus stamped on his coins) was first quoted by Thomas Lodge in 1590, and its English version was later equated (by Samuel Butler in the seventeenth century) with the now more familiar "haste makes waste."

Conspicuous by His Absence

[In A.D. 22,] Junia, sixty-three years after the battle of Philippi, reached the
end of her days; Cato was her maternal uncle, and she was the wife of
Cassius and the sister of Brutus. Her will was the subject of much specula-
tion among the crowd, since, though she named nearly every one of the
leading men, and in high terms, she omitted to mention Tiberius. This he
accepted decently; and he did not prohibit the funeral from proceeding
with a eulogy at the rostrum and all the other customary solemnities. The
effigies of twenty very distinguished families were borne before her . . . .
But Cassius and Brutus were most conspicuous, precisely because their
effigies were not to be seen.

Tacitus, The Annals of Imperial Rome, Book 3, paragraph 76

Lord John Russell (1792–1878)—sometime prime minister of
Great Britain and grandfather of the philosopher Bertrand
Russell—was famous for turning out the quotable phrase. His
1859 address to the Electors of the City of London was memorable for one coinage in particular: "conspicuous by its absence"
(he was referring to a provision lacking in a reform bill). But Lord
Russell later denied authorship, attributing the phrase to one of
his favorite historians, the Roman chronicler Tacitus.

Tacitus doesn't put it quite the way Russell did, but he comes

very close, in a description of the funeral of Junia Tertulla. Junia was the sister of Marcus Brutus (one of Julius Caesar's assassins), the wife of Cassius (Brutus's co-conspirator), and the niece of Cato of Utica (one of Caesar's most prominent enemies). Though she died sixty-three years after Marc Antony defeated Brutus and Cassius at Philippi in 44 B.C., her relatives' crimes had not been forgotten. The emperor Tiberius, a rather touchy individual, might have been expected to bear a particular grudge, since his stepfather was Caesar Augustus, Julius's nephew. Furthermore, Junia had conspicuously omitted to praise Tiberius in her will.

But in a rare show of restraint, Tiberius allowed Junia a ceremonial funeral. Most conspicuous among the attendees were her brother and husband—conspicuous, that is, by the absence of their statues. Tacitus's ironic remark is the source of Lord Russell's phrase, and thus the ultimate source of many later quotations, many of them equally ironic. O. Henry, for example, in his story "A Municipal Report," describes this examination of the body of a certain Major Wentworth Caswell: "A doctor was testing him for the immortal ingredient. His decision was that it was conspicuous by its absence." In a scathing review of the works of the now-forgotten novelist Mrs. Humphrey Ward, William Lyon Phelps judged that "The principle of selection—so important a part of all true art—is conspicuous only by its absence."

An Arbiter of Taste

Petronius slept by day and dispatched the duties and pleasures of life by night; where others strove for fame by industry, Petronius sought it by sloth. . . . However, as proconsul of Bithynia, and soon after as consul, he showed himself vigorous and equal to his business. Then, sinking back into his vices, or perhaps into an imitation of them, he was gathered up into Nero's inner circle, as Arbiter of Taste; for a time, the emperor thought nothing charming or delicate unless Petronius had approved it.

Tacitus, *The Annals of Imperial Rome*, Book 16, chapter 18

Petronius seems to be in luck when Nero calls him to Rome to serve as the first official *elegantiae arbiter*—the emperor's "arbiter of taste." As governor of Bithynia (in northwest Asia Minor, now in Turkish Anatolia) the pleasure-loving Petronius had found himself far removed from the heart of the action. But subsequent events will make him envy those laid-back days.

For starters, Nero was legendarily tasteless, and what he is looking for in an arbiter is someone who will applaud his gaucheries and his embarrassingly bad poetizing. To make matters worse, another of Nero's favorites, Tigellinus, envying Petronius "as a rival and a more expert hedonist," falsely accuses the arbiter of plotting against his employer. Nero arrests Petronius, who promptly slits his wrists, well aware of the emperor's capacity for cruelty. Petronius was probably better off for it.

"Petronius Arbiter," as he has become known, is probably the Petronius who wrote the satirical novel *The Satyricon*—not a work everyone has found to be in good taste [*see* ONE HAND WASHES THE OTHER].

Nero Fiddled While Rome Burned

Nero, in Antium at the time, did not return to the city until the fire drew nigh to the house he had built connecting the Palatine to the Gardens of Maecenas. Yet it was not possible to extinguish it, and thus the Palatine, the house, and everything nearby were consumed. . . . [Afterward, Nero did what he could to relieve the homeless and hungry], yet these efforts, however popular in intent, proved vain; for the rumor was spreading that at the very time the city was burning, Nero had mounted his private stage and had sung the destruction of Troy, thus assimilating past calamities to present evils.

Tacitus, *The Annals of Imperial Rome,* Book 15, chapter 39

Does Nero really "fiddle while Rome burns"? In Tacitus's version of the tale, in A.D. 64 the Emperor Nero climbs on a stage and sings while the worst fire in Rome's history rages about him. (Suetonius even accuses him of starting the fire because there were too many ugly old buildings.) Apparently, Nero performs a scene out of Greek epic for his decadent hangers-on, comparing the conflagration that engulfed a defeated Troy to the raging inferno that is Rome in its decline.

Nero, you will note, does not "fiddle" while Rome burns; the fiddle, in fact, wasn't invented until the middle ages. Tacitus doesn't even lend full credence to the rumor that Nero sang the destruction of Troy. Other versions of the legend, however, do have Nero singing with a lyre, a stringed instrument closer to the harp than to the violin.

The first reference in English writing to Nero's fiddling appears to date to the mid-seventeenth century. By that time, the verb "to fiddle" was already associated with frivolous or vain activity.

Money Doesn't Smell

Vespasian affected a kind of sarcasm toward his unseemly gain and filthy
lucre, as if by scoffing he might mitigate their odium and make a joke out
of them. . . . When his son Titus found fault with him for managing to
derive tribute even out of urine, he held up to his son's nose some coins out
of the first payment, and asked whether the smell was offensive. When
Titus answered "No," Vespasian replied: "And yet it comes of urine."

Suetonius, *The Deified Vespasian*, paragraph 23

I'm not sure this incident is sufficient to prove it, but the
Emperor Vespasian was generally thought to be quite a witty
man. He is better known today for his efficient administration,
which lasted from A.D. 70 to 79. Vespasian is, or should be, dear
to the hearts of tourists, since it was he who got the Colosseum
under way, in addition to building or restoring other famous
Roman structures.

As the son of a tax collector, Vespasian had an interesting
relationship to money. He was always demanding his cut, while
at the same time jesting about his own petty greed. His son
Titus, who would be the next emperor, on occasion expressed
his embarrassment, but Vespasian was nonplussed. When Titus
objects to his father's tax on public urinals, Vespasian delivers a
reply that later became famous. The traditional summary of
Suetonius's account is "*pecunia non olet*"—"money doesn't smell."
Or, as Juvenal puts it in his "Fourteenth Satire," "Money smells
good no matter where it comes from." A modern American
version of this classical phrase might be, "It's green, isn't it?"
Money might be made from the most unsavory business, but
afterward it tells no tales.

MISCELLANEOUS

I have included in this section those phrases that don't fit into any of the other sections, whether because they're attributable to no one author, because they don't fall under the rubrics of "drama," "history" or "philosophy," or because their authors have contributed fewer than three entries. Some of these writers are actually quite famous—Ovid, for example, is vastly more important to the development of English literature than is Pliny the Elder. But Ovid's exact expressions have proved less lasting than the tales he told or the style in which he told them.

For biographies of the authors and personages cited in this section, refer to the glossary which begins on p. 211.

An Achilles' Heel

For the sake of your glory and the future delights of youth,
If on your account I suffered the earth and a lowly husband,
If I armed you at birth with the severe waters of the Styx—
    Would it had been all of you!—
Take for a while these secure coverings, which will not harm your spirit.

Statius, *Achilleid*, Book 1, lines 267–271

Achilles hasn't always had an Achilles' heel. True, he's always had a weak spot, but in Homer's original tale (in the *Iliad*), it's Achilles' pride; according to later tellings, it is his love for the Trojan princess Polyxena. Ovid suggested, in his *Metamorphoses*, that Achilles has a vulnerable spot on his body, but the Latin poet Statius was the first to imply that it is Achilles' heel.

According to Statius (ca. A.D. 45–96), Achilles' mother Thetis, a sea-nymph, hopes to prevent her infant son's fated death at an early age by dipping him in the Styx (a poisonous underworld river), whose waters render him proof against any mortal wound. Unfortunately, as Thetis baptizes Achilles, she holds him by the heel, which thus remains unbathed.

It took another 1700 years for the phrase "Achilles' heel" to make its way into English. Samuel Taylor Coleridge provides the earliest traced occurrence, when he refers to Ireland as "that vulnerable heel of the British Achilles" (*The Friend*, 1810). Carlyle coined "Achilles'-heel" in 1864, and George Bernard Shaw applied it in a letter of 1897: "Divorce is the Achilles heel of marriage." The legend also spawned the medical term *tendo Achillis*, or "Achilles' tendon," which attaches the calf muscles to the heel, and which is, as most of us have painfully realized, quite vulnerable indeed.

Just as our metaphor refers to the fatally weak point of an otherwise unassailable force or plan, Achilles' own heel provided a deadly opening to his enemies. In the late versions of his story, Achilles falls prey to a poisoned arrow, launched by the Trojan prince Paris at the instigation of Neptune and Apollo, gods who opposed the Greeks in the Trojan War [*see* p. 3]. While it is foretold in Homer's version that Achilles will be slain by Paris and Apollo, there is no mention of how this eventually came about.

To Add Insult to Injury

A fly bit the bare head of a bald man, who, trying to swat it, gave himself a slap. Then the fly said, laughing, "You would avenge the bite of so small a creature by killing him; and so you would add insult to injury by striking yourself?" The man replied: "It is easy to be reconciled with myself, because I know that I had no intention of hurting myself. But you, tiny creature of a despised race, beastly animal, who takes pleasure in sucking human blood, I would like to kill you, even at the price of committing a greater evil."

Phaedrus, "The Bald Man and the Fly"

The Roman fabulist Phaedrus (ca. 15 B.C.–A.D. 50), employing the phrase "to add insult to injury," seems to be drawing on a well-known proverb, but his fly offers the first exact rendering of it. (Cicero had written "to add damage to injury," and Horace came close with "to add outrage to damage.") But our usage—which dates from the mid-eighteenth century—differs from that of Phaedrus's jolly fly. Today, one insults the person he has already injured; the bald man of the fable insults himself when he would injure the fly.

It seems that Phaedrus, who was the Aesop of the Roman Empire, was no stranger to either insult or injury. A younger contemporary describes him as a "shameless jester," though his fables reveal a man of moral seriousness. That some found his writings insulting, however, is clear; Sejanus, right-hand man of the emperor Tiberius, detected veiled political allegory in Phaedrus's books, and the fabulist was punished. He wrote "The Bald Man and the Fly" after these events, so perhaps the jocose insect is something of a self-portrait. If so, the bumbling retribution of the bald man might allude to Sejanus's retribution, but then Phaedrus's moral—deliberate injuries deserve harsh punishment—would be oddly masochistic.

The Calendar

It took the Romans a while to figure out how to properly account for time. Certain Greek states—each with its own calendar—had more or less successfully negotiated the relationship of twelve lunar months to one solar year. But the Romans started out with a calendar that lacked two months—the ones now called January and February. The problem was partially corrected by the Republican era in Rome, but somebody (probably some committee) botched the whole thing up by adding a "leap month" between February 23 and February 24. When Caesar came to power, the calendar was thus well out of whack with the solar cycle, and he set about to reconcile them in 46 B.C., instituting what became known as the "Julian calendar."

This calendar, a compromise between the Republican calendar and the Egyptian solar calendar, is similar to our own, except for the fact that March, rather than January, was the first month of the year. (January wasn't promoted until Pope Gregory XIII proclaimed its precedence in 1582, a promotion ignored in England until the eighteenth century.) Some months were simply numbered—*Sextilis* ("sixth"), for example, now called August—but others were already named after various gods. Here's a summary of where the names of our months come from.

JANUARY—Supposed to have been introduced, along with February, by Numa Pompilius, second king of Rome, January is named after Januar, festival of Janus, the ancient Latin god of gates and later of all beginnings. It has been supposed, then, that January was to have been the first month of the year, but fell victim to political machinations. But it is equally likely that the month earned its name simply by virtue of including Januar.

FEBRUARY—February is derived from *februum*, a Roman ritual of purification, and ultimately from the old Latin verb *februare*, "to purify." In particular, the festival of Lupercalia, held on what is now February 15, involved simultaneous ritual sacrifices (to Lupercus, god of fertility) and ritual purifications.

MARCH—The month in which spring begins, long the first month of the year, is named after the god Mars. You might think Mars, whom we know as the god of war, would have little to do with the beginning of everybody's favorite season. But when the Romans inherited this god from the indigenous peoples, he was the god of agriculture; only later did he also become the god of war.

APRIL—"April" seems to derive from *aperire*, "to open, reveal, uncover." There's no certain account of this etymology, but perhaps the reference is to the way flowers open in springtime, or to the tendency of people to uncover themselves at the first hint of nice weather.

MAY—May takes its name from the goddess Maia, a daughter of the Titan Atlas and mother of Mercury by Jupiter. It is uncertain why this month was consecrated to Maia, since we have only scanty evidence of her significance to the Romans; by some accounts she was a goddess of growth.

JUNE—June derives from the Latin *Junonius*, which in turn derives from the older Italian form *Uni*, for Juno, queen of the gods. The month, however, isn't directly named after the goddess, but rather after a prominent Roman family, the Junius clan, which seems to have been honored by the divine reference.

JULY—Originally *Quinctilis*, "the fifth month," July was renamed, at Marc Antony's instigation, in honor of Julius Caesar, crosser of the Rubicon, first sole dictator of Rome, and reformer of the calendar. This was just as good as renaming the month after a god, since Caesar was in fact posthumously deified, as were all subsequent emperors.

AUGUST—What was good enough for Caesar was good enough for his nephew and successor, born Caius Octavius but posthumously christened "Augustus" ("reverend," "magnificent") by the Roman senate in A.D. 27. The same compliant senate proclaimed that the month formerly known as *Sixtilis* ("sixth") should thenceforth be known as Augustus, and we too have complied, absent the Latin suffix.

SEPTEMBER, OCTOBER, NOVEMBER, DECEMBER—Boring, boring, boring, boring. These months saw no benefit from later Roman senates, who perhaps balked at the thought of having to date their letters with the names of the despised emperors Tiberius, Caligula, Claudius, and Nero. (They almost renamed October after Domitian, yet another despot.) So we're stuck with the original names, which mean seventh, eighth, ninth, and tenth, respectively.

To Err Is Human, to Forgive Divine

Demonax was never known to shout or be overly vehement or angry, even when he had to correct someone; he touched offenses, but pardoned offenders, saying that one should model oneself after doctors, who treat sickness but are not angry with the sick. He thought that to err is human, but divine (in gods or men) to put the error right.

Lucian, *Demonax*, paragraph 7

It is well to keep in mind that nothing is said that has not been said before [*see* p. 129]. Those who make a point of citing sources quote "To err is human, to forgive, divine" and confidently credit Alexander Pope's *An Essay on Criticism* (1711) as the source. It is true that Pope's is the first English version, and is indeed the one we remember. But he seems to have been reading his Lucian, and maybe he expected his contemporaries to recognize the allusion. Perhaps, too, he would be appalled that we assume he is the inventor of the phrase. But perhaps not: to err is, after all, human.

Lucian himself attributes the saying to Demonax of Cyprus, one of his mentors. (The basic idea, however, appears much earlier; Menander, for example, had written, "Being human, I erred.") Lucian portrays Demonax as an almost superhuman individual, utterly beyond reproach, a fine speaker, a true lover of philosophy, modest, charming, and responsible, a man of enduring spirit and honest generosity. Perhaps it takes a man so nearly divine to appreciate how human it is to err. Though it might be said that Demonax anticipated the Christian precept that one should condemn the sin while forgiving the sinner, note that what Demonax actually says is not that to *forgive* is divine, but rather that to *correct* is divine. Being so much harder than merely condescending to forgive, healing the sinner is rather more divine than divine.

Half Is More Than the Whole

Let justice guide us in our contention, Perses, and the counsels of Zeus—
not as before, when as we divided our lands you avariciously seized the
better part, and the bribe-devouring lords unjustly granted you more than
was your right. O blind fools, whose erring souls know not that the half is
more than the whole, and that mallow and asphodel are wholesome.

Hesiod, *Works and Days*, lines 34–41

While the word "I" almost never appears in Homer's works
outside quotation marks, in his *Works and Days* the slightly later
poet Hesiod (eighth century B.C.) is not so modest. This poem,
which is a versified lecture on the working life, begins with a
settling of personal accounts. It appears that Hesiod's brother
Perses was not content with an equal division of their patrimony,
so he bribed the authorities to sanction his seizure of the better
part of his father's estate. The helpless Hesiod took the only
revenge he could by upbraiding in poetry both his brother and
the "bribe-devouring lords."

As Hesiod sees it, these "fools" don't understand that "the
half is more than the whole"—that is, that less is more if more
must be obtained unjustly. The hard-working Hesiod is better
off with his "mallow and asphodel" (simple fare) than his
arrogant betters with their ill-gotten gains. Perses has not really
benefited from his windfall; rather, it has led him into dissolute
ways, while impoverished Hesiod has learned how to preserve
what little he has. Hesiod's proverb has been often quoted, in
Greek (Plato calls it "a most true saying"), in Latin, and, at least
since the revival of ancient literature in the sixteenth century, in
English. Its usual meaning is "be content with modesty, because
greed will get you nowhere."

To Lead by the Nose

The only certain ground for discovering truth is the faculty of discriminating false from true, distinguishing the sound and genuine from the base and counterfeit, as the silver assayers do with coins. When you have at last managed to acquire such a faculty, then you may investigate the [Stoic] doctrines. Otherwise, I can assure you, you will be led by the nose by anyone who chooses to do it, and you will run after anything they hold out to you, as cattle do after a green bough.

Lucian, Hermotimus, paragraph 68

Lucian's dialogue *Hermotimus* offers the earliest literary record of the phrase that became in English "to lead by the nose." He probably refers to the contemporary method of transporting bears—by dragging them from a nose-ring.

In this long and rather tedious dialogue, the skeptic Lycinus bludgeons the title character so that he will abandon his Stoic views [*see* STOIC]. Lycinus's strategy is to show Hermotimus that it's so difficult as to be impossible to really know false Stoic doctrine from true, so the whole enterprise should simply be given up. Unless Hermotimus is fully armed against false teaching, he will be "dragged by the nose" by frauds.

The first English quotation dates to 1581, used to describe what deceiving Papists are able to do with gullible innocents. John Florio translated an Italian equivalent in 1598, and soon thereafter Shakespeare put the phrase in the mouth of Iago, who is convinced that Othello "will as tenderly be led by the nose/As asses are" (*Othello*, Act 1, scene 3). He's right.

The Musical Modes

"And which are the harmonies expressive of sorrow? . . ."

"The harmonies which you mean are the mixed or tenor Lydian [Mixolydian], and the full-toned or bass Lydian [Syntonolydian], and such like."

"These then," I said, "must be banished; even to women who have a character to maintain they are of no use, and much less to men. . . . In the next place, drunkenness and softness and indolence are utterly unbecoming the character of our guardians."

"Utterly unbecoming."

"And which are the soft or drinking harmonies?"

"The Ionian," he replied, "and the Lydian; they are termed 'relaxed.'"

"Well, and are these of any military use?"

"Quite the reverse," he replied; "and if so the Dorian and the Phrygian are the only ones which you have left."

Plato, *Republic*, Book 3

Plato's catalogue of musical scales or "modes" is one of the earliest to survive, and it gives us a more or less complete list of the prevailing harmonic modes at the height of Greek culture. And despite the fact that the scales and intervals of modern Western music significantly differ from what must have been those of ancient Greek music, we continue to use today all the terms Plato mentions, with one exception ("Syntonolydian").

The plaintive LYDIAN and MIXOLYDIAN modes—today equivalent to playing the white keys on a piano, beginning with F and G respectively—are named after Lydia, an ancient kingdom in Asia Minor (now Turkey). You may recall Lydia as the country ruled, and brought to ruin, by the very wealthy king Croesus [*see* RICH AS CROESUS]. Mixolydian literally means "half-Lydian"; Syntonolydian means "tight or intense Lydian," which is sometimes taken to be the plain Lydian, as opposed to the Mixolydian. But Plato seems to distinguish the Syntonolydian from the Lydian, and he may mean by the former what we call today the Aeolian mode—the white keys beginning with A (the minor scale). In any case, Plato doesn't like any of them.

The IONIAN mode—now equivalent to playing the white keys beginning with C (the major scale)—is named after Ionia, a region of Greek settlement on the Aegean coast of Asia Minor. Readers should be happy to note that Plato considers effeminate what is now the principal harmonic mode of all Western music.

The DORIAN mode—approximated by playing the white keys beginning with D—derives its name from Doris, another Greek settlement on the Aegean coast of Asia Minor, south of Ionia. This mode fares a little better in Plato's estimation, and was known for its solemn character. As Plutarch says, "Plato . . . chose the Dorian, as that which is most beseeming valiant, sober, and temperate men."

The PHRYGIAN mode—play the white keys beginning with E—takes its name from the Kingdom of Phrygia in Asia Minor, home to the beguiling river Meander [*see* p. 35]. This mode was thought best suited to working up aggressive passions. John Playford, in his *Brief Introduction to the Skill of Music* (1674), reports that "The Phrygian mode was a more warlike and courageous kind of music, expressing the music of trumpets and other instruments of old, exciting to arms."

Plato is dead set on censoring all the modes except the Dorian and Phrygian: in his ideal Republic, no relaxing music is permitted. Aristotle is a little more tolerant, but like Plato he believes that music is more than a harmless diversion. In his *Politics* he says that "music has a power of forming the character," and is therefore to be allowed in the education of children. To his mind, however, the warlike Phrygian mode is not so suitable to cultivating the character, and he settles on the Dorian as the best of all possible modes.

One Hand Washes the Other

The only one to show any spunk was a Thracian, and he only fought when we tarred him on. In the end they all got a sound thrashing; in fact the crowd demanded that every one of them be soundly whipped, they were obviously such arrant runaways. "Anyhow I gave you a show," said he. "And I applauded," said I; "reckon it up, and I gave you more than I got. One hand washes the other."

Petronius, *Satyricon*, paragraph 45

At a rowdy banquet, a group of Roman citizens discourse on such weighty topics as the gladiator show a few days hence [*see* THUMBS UP/THUMBS DOWN]. The rag-seller Echion here weighs the past performances of a rather mongrel bunch of gladiators in the service of the private citizen Norbanus, and finds them lacking. Norbanus insists that he at least put on a show; Echion replies that derisive "applause" was exactly what it deserved: "One hand washes the other."

The more familiar English equivalent of this phrase is "one good turn deserves another," which is actually how Oscar Wilde rendered it in the translation of Petronius I've adapted here. "One good turn asketh another" turns up in English by 1400, while "one hand washes the other" doesn't appear until the sixteenth century. But Petronius borrows from an ancient Greek proverb, "one hand washes the other, and finger helps finger." The idea is a bit strange, since it requires thinking of each hand as having an independent will and its own agenda—as if there were the possibility that your right hand might decide not to reciprocate after the left hand has washed it. And it is difficult to see how one hand might wash the other when both are busy mocking applause.

One Man's Meat Is Another's Poison

In order that you may understand why different food suits different creatures, and why what is foul and bitter to some may nevertheless seem very sweet to others, I will explain. There is in these things so great a diversity and difference that one man's food is another's sharp poison. And thus there is a serpent that, when touched by a man's saliva, dies by chewing and consuming itself.

Lucretius, *De Rerum Natura*, lines 633–639

Titus Lucretius Carus (94–55 B.C.) was the chief Latin exponent of Epicurean philosophy [*see* p. 59], and here he attempts to explain the human condition in terms of Epicurus's "atomism"—the philosophy that creation stems from the natural combination of an infinite number of atoms, rather than from the acts of invisible gods.

That "one man's food is another's sharp poison" Lucretius chalks up to differences in atomic structure. Simply put, just as we differ from animals in outward form, so too do our tongues and palates differ from theirs. Food composed of soft, round atoms is pleasing to the human palate, but will disagree with certain animal tongues, which are composed of rougher stuff. Likewise, different people are equipped with different tastebuds, which may also be roughed up by diseases and distempers: so it's no mystery that one man's meat is another's poison.

Lucretius, you will note, is not actually talking about different people's opinions (or meat in particular) when he coins this famous phrase. He's talking about an actual fact of nature, and he had occasion to better understand the literal truth of his words. According to legend, as reported by St. Jerome for example, he fell victim to his own philosophy, poisoned with a love potion.

To See and Be Seen

As a long train of grain-bearing ants frequently comes and goes,
    Bearing the usual food in their mouths,
Or as bees, having reached the woodlands or the fragrant pasture,
    Fly through the flowers and above the thyme,
So rush the most elegant women to the crowded shows:
    Often has the throng impeded my judgment.
They come to see, and they come to be seen:
    That place is the ruin of chaste decency.

Ovid, The Art of Love, lines 93–100

What the singles bar and trendy nightclub are today, the theater
and the public games were in Ovid's time. Even the poet's head
spins at the shows, where elegant women gather to "see and be
seen"—our modification of a phrase Ovid coins. With tongue
somewhere in cheek, Ovid calls the public games "the ruin of
chaste decency"—whether of the women's decency or of his
own is unclear.

Once again, Chaucer was the English pioneer; the Wife of
Bath, while her husband is in London, "had the better leisure for
to play,/ And for to see, and eke for to be seen/ Of lusty folk." By
"lusty" the frolicsome wife means something like "vibrant," but
her word choice is apt to Ovid's point. People aren't coming to
the theaters just to look at one another.

"To see and be seen" itself first appears in Ben Jonson's
"Epithalamion" (1609), a wedding poem: in the procession, the
young folk are all pranked up, "As they came all to see and to be
seen!" Though we expect these youth to behave themselves as
befits a marriage ceremony, the amorous element is still present;
not so with many later uses of the phrase. Increasingly, what is
on display is not one's charm, but one's wealth—if the two may
be properly distinguished.

The Tongue Is Sharper Than the Sword

Do not be carried away in your heart by the delights of bold talk.
Practice the art of speaking, which will profit everyone greatly.
Speech is for man a sharper weapon than the sword;
God has given each being one weapon: to birds,
The ability to fly; to coursers, speed; to lions, strength;
To bulls, horns which grow of themselves; to bees, he has given
Their sting as a natural defense; to men, the armor of words.

PSEUDO-PHOCYLIDES, *Wise Sayings*, lines 122–128

While Edward George Bulwer-Lytton, Baron Lytton gets credit for the line, "the pen is mightier than the sword," he didn't invent the idea. At best, he updated a classical proverb coined before the pen had been invented.

Whoever wrote these lines—anonymous but once attributed to Phocylides of Miletus (sixth century B.C.)—doesn't use the word "tongue." Rather, he says that *logos* is sharper than the sword. Now, *logos* is a pretty complicated word, meaning a variety of things in Greek—from "speech" to "reason." In fact, for the Greeks speech *was* reason—or at least the potential to be reasonable. Armed with *logos*, man, among all beings, is capable of defending himself and gaining objectives without recourse to violence. But effective speech requires practice, and you should make especially sure to guard against bold and arrogant talk, or else the sharpness of your tongue might provoke others to take up the sword.

This leads to another idea: "The tongue is not steel, but it cuts," runs an English proverb. The gods may have armed us with *logos*, but they put a weapon in our mouths that we often have a hard time controlling.

There's No Place Like Rome

If the Greeks and Romans had got around to developing intellectual property law, it would be a lot easier today to trace famous phrases back to their authors. I've made do with others' testimony and my own deductions in compiling the main entries of this book, but some phrases refuse to be pinned down. "To be afraid of your own shadow," for example, definitely shows up in Plato's dialogue *Phaedo*, but he quotes it as a proverbial saying; so I can only attribute it to "anonymous." I've included a selection of such sayings in this appendix, along with second-rank phrases that didn't make the cut for inclusion in the main text (for example, "Evil communications corrupt good manners"). Also included are post-classical phrases that many of us might have assumed were on the tip of every Roman's tongue—such as "All roads lead to Rome."

"ALL ROADS LEAD TO ROME" was perhaps true when the Romans were building all the roads, but the phrase doesn't appear before the French poet Jean de la Fontaine recorded it in a fable published in 1694 (*"Tous chemins vont à Rome"*); Voltaire repeated the phrase in a letter to another Fontaine in 1750. Though Chaucer had written "diverse paths lead diverse folk the right way to Rome," the first occurrence of the actual phrase in English dates to 1872.

"ALTER EGO," the Latin for "another I," has no psychological import when it is found in classical texts. The younger Seneca, for example, uses it rather literally when he asks, "What is sweeter than to have a friend with whom you may boldly speak of everything? Such a friend is rarely found, and should be diligently kept, for he is another self [*alter ego*]" (*On Morals*). (Latin writers seem to have adapted the Greek phrase *allos ego*, which is attributed by Diogenes Laertius to Zeno of Citium. Aristotle uses a similar expression in his *Ethics*, Book 9.) R. Layton, in the first recorded use of "alter ego" in English, is similarly literal, and may even have Seneca in mind when he advises that "Ye must have such as ye may trust even as well as your own self, which must be unto you as *alter ego*" (1537). Oddly enough, "ego" by itself doesn't appear in English until the late eighteenth century, and then as merely a humorous substitute for "I" or "self"; only later did it take on the meanings "interior consciousness," "self-esteem," and, after Freud, "psychic identity." Similarly, "alter ego" has only in this century been used to mean "an alternate identity of the same person" as well as "another person closely identified with the self."

"To BEG THE QUESTION" is a phrase used by Aristotle in his *Prior Analytics* (ca. 340 B.C.), where he defines it as "to assume the original question" and as one sort of "failure to demonstrate the required proposition." The proverbial form of the Greek expression was translated into Latin as *petitio principii*, a phrase still used in some (usually pedantic) English writings.

"DRINK TO ME ONLY WITH THINE EYES" begins Ben Jonson's poem "To Celia," published in 1616. Jonson lifted the conceit from a classical love-letter by Flavius Philostratus (b. ca. A.D. 170), who compares a woman's eyes to drinking cups and fantasizes sipping from them. Pretty disgusting.

"EVIL COMMUNICATIONS CORRUPT GOOD MANNERS" should be familiar to students of the Bible—it's one of St. Paul's warnings to the Corinthians (I Corinthians 15:33). (What the saint means is "bad company leads to bad habits.") But Paul had been brushing up his classics—he is directly quoting a line from Menander's play *Thais*, of which only fragments now survive.

"THE FACE THAT LAUNCHED A THOUSAND SHIPS" is a highly quotable description of Helen of Troy's aspect, as well as of her unfortunate fate; but the phrase wasn't coined until twenty-three centuries after Homer, by Christopher Marlowe in his play *Doctor Faustus* (1588), in which Helen makes a cameo appearance. Marlowe probably recalled one of Lucian's *Dialogues of the Dead*, in which "a thousand ships from the Greek union" are mentioned in a description of Helen.

"TO FALL ON ONE'S SWORD" was the Roman way to avoid the indignity of capture. Several of the notables mentioned in this book—Cato of Utica, Brutus, and Marc Antony, for example— elected to end their own lives in this fashion rather than be paraded about in an enemy's triumph.

"FAMILIARITY BREEDS CONTEMPT" was a Latin proverb, and is recorded by Publilius Syrus. Though he doesn't use the phrase, Aesop was the first to demonstrate the idea, in his fable "The Fox and the Lion": a fox who has never seen a lion meets one and is terrified; a second encounter proves a bit less frightening; the third time the fox, far from being afraid, strikes up a familiar conversation with the lion. This isn't "contempt" in the sense of "scorn," but in the sense of "fearlessness." In one of Aesop's more ironic tales, the lion would respond to the fox's boldness by eating him.

"FANATIC," according to the simplest etymology, derives from the Latin *fanum*, "temple." But the meaning "zealous" or "zealot" seems to derive from the peculiar behavior of priests who served the Roman war goddess Bellona at a *fanum* built by the military dictator Sulla in the first century B.C. Every year the priests staged a festival during which they tore off their robes and hacked at themselves with axes, splattering blood everywhere. This behavior could only be a sign of divine inspiration, and so *fanaticus* came to mean something like "crazed by the gods." When the word "fanatic" first appeared in English in the sixteenth century, it meant "crazed person," and then more specifically "possessed with divine fury." "Religious maniac" is still the principal meaning of the term, but in the shortened form "fan" it also means simply "devotee" or "adherent."

"FOREWARNED, FOREARMED" was a Latin proverb: *Praemonitus, praemunitus.*

"HABIT IS SECOND NATURE" is a saying attributed to practically every classical philosopher, but is said to have been especially favored by Diogenes the Cynic. Aristotle, in his *Nicomachean Ethics* (Book 7), attributes the phrase to Evenus, who wrote epigrams in the sixth century B.C., and invokes the idea in his *Rhetoric* (Book 1). Cicero too was fond of the notion, as he quotes it in several places.

"HEART OF STONE" is, unsurprisingly, an ancient saying, found for example in Homer's *Odyssey* (Book 23), where Telemachus accuses his mother of having a "heart that is harder than stone" ("heart of iron" is actually Homer's more frequent expression). In the second century B.C., the Latin poet Ennius opined that "there are many with hearts of stone." Homer also seems to have been the first to suggest the phrase "heart in one's mouth," when in Book 22 of the *Iliad* Hector's wife Andromache is seized with fear; she confesses to her maids that "My heart, rising up, beats in my mouth." Petronius Arbiter comes closer to the modern phrasing in his novel The *Satyricon*, but it first appears in English in the anonymous play *Thersites* (1537), based on a character out of Homer's *Iliad*.

"HISTORY REPEATS ITSELF" is a proverb attributed to an obscure nineteenth-century writer, Augustus Jessopp, but Thucydides expresses the same idea in Book 1 of his *History of the Peloponnesian War*: "what has happened will, given human nature, happen again in the future, and in much the same way."

"THE LESSER EVIL" appears frequently in classical texts, for example in Plato's *Protagoras:* "when a man is compelled to choose one of two evils, no one will choose the greater when he might have the lesser evil." Aristotle quotes it as a proverb in his *Nicomachean Ethics* (Books 2 and 5), as does Cicero in *Of Duties* (Book 3). In English, the standard versions of the phrase, from Chaucer's time to the nineteenth century, were "Of two evils choose the least" and the more grammatical "Of two evils choose the less."

"LET THE BUYER BEWARE"—or, in Latin, *caveat emptor*—derives from a legal maxim of uncertain date, and is not quoted in surviving English literature before 1523. The full text is "Let the buyer beware, for he ought not be ignorant of the nature of the property he is buying from another." The more general English word "caveat," a noun derived from the Latin predicate "let him beware," now means "precaution" or "warning," and is also a legal term for a motion filed to postpone a court proceeding until the petitioner is heard.

"LOVE IS BLIND," a proverb first recorded in English by Chaucer (*The Merchant's Tale*, 1598), seems to have been popular with the Romans. We have no first source, but Plautus alludes to it in his play *The Braggart Warrior* (211 B.C.), and many later authors—such as Horace, Ovid, and Catullus—employ phrases like "blind love," "blind desire," and "blind self-love." In Western literature (Shakespeare's *Two Gentlemen of Verona*, for example), the expression tends to be associated with images of little blind Cupid aiming his golden arrow at some victim; but Cupid's blindness seems to be a post-classical invention.

"TO MAKE A VIRTUE OF NECESSITY" is approximated by the Latin rhetorician Quintilian (b. ca. A.D. 40), who writes in his *Institutes of Oratory* that "We give to necessity the praise of virtue"; but the English cliché more directly derives from an expression of St. Jerome (d. A.D. 420): *facis de necessitate virtutem*, "You make a virtue of necessity." The English, adapted from an Old French version, first shows up in Chaucer's *Troilus and Criseyde* (ca. 1374).

"THE MOUNTAINS HAVE BROUGHT FORTH A MOUSE," a humorous comment on grand advertisements for the essentially frivolous, derives from the fable "A Mountain in Labor," attributed to Aesop. As the story goes, a mountain rumbles as if it is ready to issue some prodigious birth; but as the local people wait in dread, the mountain brings forth only a "ridiculous mouse." Horace, in his *Ars Poetica*, draws the moral that big boasts are liable to make you a bigger fool.

"A NECESSARY EVIL" seems to derive from a few lines in Euripides' tragedy *Orestes* (ca. 410 B.C.): "To the sick the couch is welcome: an evil place, yet necessary." Those of us who always welcome the couch might wonder why the sick would find it evil, but the Greeks abhorred even necessary idleness. Later, Menander would inspire a more common proverb when he wrote, in one of his unidentified fragments, that "Marriage, if one will face the truth,/ Is an evil, but a necessary evil." Many still find marriage evil, but these days its necessity seems a bit dubious. Menander's phrase was quoted in English by 1547, and as late as 1721 it was still proverbial that "wives and wind are necessary evils." Tom Paine decisively divorced "necessary evil" from marriage in 1776 when he wrote, in *Common Sense*, that "Government, even in its best state, is but a necessary evil; in its worst state, an intolerable one."

"THERE'S NO ACCOUNTING FOR TASTES" derives from the Latin saying, *De gustibus non est disputandum*—"One cannot argue with tastes."

"OUT OF SIGHT, OUT OF MIND," quoted in English by the mid-fifteenth century, seems to have been in the Greek and Roman air. Homer approximates it in his *Odyssey* (Book 1), where Telemachus, referring to his father Odysseus, says, "out of sight, out of remembrance." In Latin, the poet Sextus Propertius wrote that "As far as love parts from sight, so far it parts from mind."

"TO PASS UNDER THE YOKE" is to undergo a ritual humiliation; the phrase derives from the ancient Roman practice of forcing defeated enemies to pass under the "yoke of ignominy," which, according to Livy (*The History of Rome*, Book 3), was made from three spears, two planted upright in the ground and the third tied across them.

"PHYSICIAN, HEAL THYSELF," a phrase we know from the Gospel according to Luke (4:23), had evidently long been a proverb in Greek and Latin (the Latin is *Medice cura teipsum*). Cicero obliquely refers to the expression in *Letters to His Friends:* "Do not imitate those bad physicians, who pretend to medical knowledge when it comes to others' ills, but who cannot heal themselves."

"TO REST ON ONE'S LAURELS" is a phrase with roots in the Greek athletic games, whose victors were awarded wreaths woven from various plants, depending on who sponsored the event. Winners of the Pythian Games, held at Pytho (later Delphi) in central Greece, garnered wreaths of laurel; those of the Olympic Games, wreaths of wild olives; and so on. And so one's "laurels" are his or her achievements. The laurel was also associated with prophetic and poetic inspiration, and thus a nation's greatest poets have ever since been called "poets laureate," even after they were no longer bestowed with a symbolic laurel crown.

"THE ROAD TO HELL IS EASY," an idea most famous from the Gospel according to Matthew (7:13—"for wide is the gate, and broad is the way, that leadeth to destruction"), was already a proverb in Rome; it appears, for example, in Virgil's *Aeneid*, Book 6: "Easy is the descent into Avernus [the Roman hell]" (it's the getting back that's hard). Diogenes Laertius ascribes the saying to the Greek philosopher Bion of Borysthenes (third century B.C.).

"A ROLLING STONE GATHERS NO MOSS" is a phrase attributed to the Roman actor Publilius Syrus (first century B.C.), who was famous for his witty apophthegms. Erasmus cites as a Greek proverb the expression "a rolling stone gathers no seaweed," which is perhaps older, but we can only speculate.

"ROSY-FINGERED DAWN" is the most famous of Homer's formulaic epithets—standard adjective-noun combinations. It first appears in Book 1 of the *Iliad* and reappears frequently; less famous though also frequent are "fair-tressed dawn" and "fair-throned dawn." Other epithets include "Zeus of the aegis" (referring to his cosmic shield); "shining-eyed Athena"; and, more familiar today, "winged words," which entered English by way of George Chapman's translation of the *Odyssey*.

"A SALARY" is what you collect at the end of the week and then spend on compact discs and car payments, but when Roman soldiers were paid their *salarium*, it was so they could purchase *sal*—Latin for "salt." (*Salarium* is the neuter form of *salarius*, "pertaining to salt." Salt was imported into Rome from the Sabine country via the *Salaria Via*.) Salt was a precious commodity then, and would have been especially important to the troops, in an era before canned food, heat-resistant chocolate bars, and refrigerators. "To be worth your salt" seems to derive from this peculiar financial arrangement, though it doesn't appear in English until the nineteenth century.

"THE SEVEN WONDERS OF THE ANCIENT WORLD" were first identified by Antipater of Sidon, a Greek writer of epigrams, in the second century B.C. He included the Pyramids of Giza, the oldest and only surviving Wonder; the Hanging Gardens of Babylon; the fifth-century B.C. Statue of Zeus at Olympia; the Temple of Artemis at Ephesus, in Asia Minor; the Mausoleum of Halicarnassus [*see* p. 41]; the Colossus of Rhodes [*see* p. 42]; and the Pharos (lighthouse) of Alexandria, erected in the third century B.C. In recent times the Iraqi government has attempted to recreate the Hanging Gardens, but their completion is uncertain.

"TO SHUDDER AT THE VERY THOUGHT" is occasionally attributed to Virgil, but not very precisely. In Book 2 of the *Aeneid*, Virgil does use the expression *horresco referens*, which literally translates as "I shudder even as I speak of it"—perhaps close enough.

"TO SMILE THROUGH TEARS" perhaps owes its origin to Homer's description of Andromache in Book 6 of the *Iliad*. The wife of Hector, Troy's greatest warrior, Andromache pleads in vain with her husband to avoid a battle she senses will be his last. Hector won't think of staying home, so Andromache attempts to put the best face on things, "smiling through tears." In Homer as in contemporary usage, the tears mean that the smile fails in its purpose.

"SOMETHING IS BETTER THAN NOTHING" was apparently a Greek proverb, a version of which surfaces in one of Menander's fragments: "Whenever you are offered only a part of something, take it; for the lesser part is better than nothing at all."

"TO SPILL SALT" has been an ominous sign since Roman times, if we are to believe the report of the scholar Sextus Pompeius Festus (second century A.D.). As we have seen [see SALARY], salt was fairly hard to come by; and Horace describes in one of his *Odes* how carefully a family guarded its salt cellar.

"TIME IS MONEY" is one of Ben Franklin's most revealing maxims, but a similar idea is attributed to the Greek philosopher Theophrastus (ca. 372–288 B.C.) by the biographer Diogenes Laertius. Theophrastus "loved to say that time is very expensive." He himself never wasted a precious minute, turning out at least 226 works in 493 volumes in his brief lifetime. Even if he began writing at age 10, that's an average of 14 volumes per year. The Athenian orator Antiphon (ca. 480–411 B.C.) is recorded as having earlier said that "the most costly outlay is the outlay of time."

"WAR IS SWEET TO THE INEXPERIENCED"—in Latin, *dulce bellum inexpertis*—first shows up, in the fifth century B.C., in one of Pindar's *Dance Songs*, in which he adds that "he that has experience of it sorely fears in his heart its approach."

"WHEN IN ROME, DO AS THE ROMANS DO" was quoted as a Latin proverb by Jeremy Taylor in the seventeenth century, but no version of it has survived the classical period. In the fourth century A.D., again according to Taylor, St. Ambrose advised St. Augustine that "If you are in Rome, live according to the Roman fashion; if you are elsewhere, live as they do there."

Glossary

ACHILLES—Legendary Greek warrior of the Trojan War; subject of a widespread hero cult in the ancient world; the sulking protagonist of Homer's *Iliad*. Achilles' spat with the Greek leader Agamemnon (over the female "prize" Briseis) results in protraction of the war, but when Achilles, with Athena's help, kills Hector, the Trojans' best man, the fight is all but over. Later accounts have it that Achilles was felled by Paris with a poisoned arrow; *see* ACHILLES' HEEL.

AENEAS—Son of the goddess Aphrodite and Trojan veteran of the war with Greece, Aeneas escaped the destruction of Troy so that he might help found Rome and star in Virgil's epic *The Aeneid*.

AESOP (sixth century B.C.)—Greek fabulist; *see* p. 23.

ALCIBIADES (ca. 450–404 B.C.)—Haughty Athenian aristocrat and general, student and "beloved" of Socrates (Alcibiades appears in Plato's *Symposium*). At turns democratic activist and suspected enemy of the city and its gods, Alcibiades, after taking part in a disastrous Athenian assault on Sicily, turned coat and fled to Sparta in 413. He was welcomed back by Athens in 407, when the city required his military genius; but a year later he was exiled, this time for good.

ALEXANDER THE GREAT (Alexander III of Macedon; 356–323 B.C.)—Son of King Philip II of Macedon, pupil of Aristotle, dreamer of world conquest. Alexander was already a military commander at age eighteen; and when his father died two years later, Alexander ensured his succession by having Philip's child by Cleopatra eliminated. Alexander consolidated Macedonia's hold on the Greek world, and then turned to Asia, finally conquering Persia and, in the meantime, Egypt and Syria; by 325 B.C., Alexander controlled a huge territory stretching to India. In India, Alexander's friend Anaxarchus, a philosopher and teacher of Pyrrhon the Skeptic, put forth to the conqueror his theory that there are an infinite number of worlds; this prompted Alexander to weep because "we have not yet become lords of a single one!" In 326 B.C. he ordered the Greeks to consider him a god; he later found an Egyptian oracle to proclaim him the son of Zeus (in his aspect as Ammon). Alexander, at the age of thirty-two, died of a fever.

ANDROMACHE—Wife of the Trojan warrior Hector in Homer's *Iliad*.

ANTIGONE—In Greek legend, a daughter of Oedipus by his mother Jocasta. When Oedipus had blinded himself and was banished from Thebes, Antigone tended to him as he wandered Greece, finally finding protection at Colonus. In Sophocles' *Antigone,* she defies Creon's order that her brother be refused the traditional burial rites, which leads Creon to imprison her in a sepulchre, where she kills herself.

ANTONY, MARC (Marcus Antonius; ca. 82–30 B.C.)—Ally of Julius Caesar in the civil war with Pompey; ally of Octavian (Augustus) after Caesar's assassination. Member of the "Second Triumvirate" with Octavian and Lepidus. Married Octavian's sister, but bolted for Cleopatra, in league with whom he skirmished with his brother-in-law. Defeated at Actium in 31 B.C.; shortly thereafter, Antony committed suicide. Antony is said to have written a book praising drunkenness.

ARCHIMEDES (ca. 287–212 B.C.)—Syracusan mathematician, scientist, and inventor. For a general account of his achievements, *see* p. 61. Archimedes died during the Roman siege of Syracuse, which the inventor helped stave off by devising machines to topple and sink enemy ships. As the story goes, Archimedes was so deeply engaged in solving a mathematical problem that he didn't even notice that the Romans had taken the city, nor did he notice when a Roman soldier cut him down.

ARISTIPPUS (fourth century B.C.)—A friend and philosophical pupil of Socrates, and thought to be the founder of the "Cyrenaic school," which advocated the pursuit of pleasure [*see* HEDONISM]. It is possible, however, that it was actually his grandson, also named Aristippus, who founded the school.

ARISTOPHANES (ca. 450–385 B.C.)—Greek dramatist and master of the "Old Comedy"; *see* p. 108.

ARISTOTLE (384–322 B.C.)—Athenian philosopher, founder of the Lyceum; the most famous of Plato's pupils; *see* p. 98.

ARRIAN (Flavius Arrianus, second century A.D.)—Governor of Cappadocia (now central Turkey) under the Roman emperor Hadrian. A pupil of the Stoic philosopher Epictetus, Arrian is best known today for his history of Alexander the Great, the *Anabasis*.

AUGUSTUS (Caius Octavius; 63 B.C.–A.D. 14)—Augustus, known in his lifetime as Caius Julius Caesar Octavianus, succeeded his great-uncle Julius Caesar as sole ruler of Rome after the collapse of the "Second Triumvirate" (Octavian, Marc Antony, Lepidus) and his defeat of Marc Antony in a civil war. Though he attempted to retain some of Rome's republican institutions, Augustus was gradually ceded supreme authority over what had become an empire, of which he was the first emperor proper. Augustus was revered in later times for administering the "*Pax Romana*," a period of peace and stability, which coincided with the golden age of Latin literature.

BELLEROPHON—Legendary Greek figure, the grandson of Sisyphus (who spent his days in Hades rolling a big stone up a hill), and son of Glaucus. When the Argive queen Anteia, desperately in love with Bellerophon, found him proof against her charms, she accused him of attempted rape; her husband, King Proteus, unwilling to avenge this alleged crime himself, then packed Bellerophon off to Anteia's father, King Iobates of Lykia, with a letter demanding that Bellerophon be put to death. Iobates devised a number of deadly tasks for our hero, all of which he survived, including his encounter with the hideous Chimera. Iobates, grudgingly admiring, marries Bellerophon to his daughter. But the gods inexplicably turn on Bellerophon—two of his children die, leaving him to wander the desolate Asian plains of Aleios. According to later accounts (such as Euripides' *Bellerophon*), the hero attempts to fly to Olympus on the winged horse Pegasus, but Zeus sets a vicious gadfly on the steed, who throws his rider from a long ways up; this is how Bellerophon ends up on Aleios where, as Homer puts it, he wanders "eating his heart out" [*see* p. 8].

BRUTUS (Marcus Junius Brutus; ca. 78–42 B.C.)—A powerful champion of republican ideals in Rome, Brutus stood with Pompey against Julius Caesar after the latter crossed the Rubicon [*see* p. 172], but later kissed and made up with the new dictator. In 44 B.C., he joined a conspiracy to assassinate Caesar, but fell in turn before the forces arrayed by Marc Antony and the young Octavian at Philippi (42 B.C.). In the face of humiliation, he took the old Roman way out and fell on his sword.

CASSIUS (Caius Cassius Longinus; d. 42 B.C.)—Cassius's career strikingly resembles Brutus's, at least in broad outline. He too stood with Pompey in the civil war and played a leading role in Caesar's assassination; he also killed himself, but beat Brutus to that punch (and had a servant insert the sword, rather than falling on it). Where Brutus was idealistic, however, Cassius was consumed with envy. Later literature, including Shakespeare's *Julius Caesar*, respects him less than his partner.

CATILINE (Lucius Sergius Catilina; d. 62 B.C.)—An extremely dangerous, though somewhat inept, Roman revolutionary, Catiline botched his governorship of Africa, and then botched a plot to murder the state consuls in 65 B.C. Yet he never gave up his desperate plots to seize power, as we are told by Cicero in a famous series of speeches. Catiline was put out of his misery in 62 B.C.

CATO OF UTICA (Marcus Porcius Cato; 95–46 B.C.)—Descendant of Cato the Censor, called "the conscience of Rome" for his fiercely republican opposition to the "First Triumvirate" of Caesar, Pompey, and Crassus. During the civil war, however, he sided with Pompey against Caesar; and when Caesar finally caught up with him, he took his own life after reading Plato's *Phaedo* (twice), in which Socrates argues that only fools do not welcome death.

CATO THE CENSOR (Marcus Porcius Cato; 234–149 B.C.)—Skilled Roman soldier and administrator who gained the post of "censor" in 184 B.C. His job, as he saw it, was to check the dissolute ways of the aristocracy and to return Rome to its traditionally austere values. He despised Greek culture as a pernicious influence on the purer Roman character, but ironically studied Greek later in life. Most famous for his saying, "Carthage must be destroyed" (*Carthago delenda est*), Cato also wrote what seems to be the first work of history in Latin, the *Origins*; he also composed the earliest surviving prose work in that language.

CATULLUS (Gaius Valerius Catullus; ca. 84–54 B.C.)—A wealthy Veronese, Catullus made his fame at Rome as a lyric poet; most notable are his erotic verses on the pseudonymous lover "Lesbia."

CHILON (sixth century B.C.)—Spartan magistrate known for austerity and strictness, one of the Seven Sages of Greece; *see* p. 77.

CHIMERA—Mythical Greek beast, described by Homer as having a goat's body, a lion's head, and a dragon's tail; she breathes fire, too. Bellerophon, intended to be just another of her victims, did away with her. Her name, deriving from the Greek for "she-goat," became in English equivalent to any fantastically horrible creature, and later to any insubstantial fancy or unfounded conception.

CICERO (Marcus Tullius Cicero; 106–43 B.C.)—Roman republican, lawyer, senator, consul, philosopher, rhetorician, and author; *see* p. 131.

CIRCE—Mythical Greek enchantress, equated in later times with witch-craft. In Homer's *Odyssey*, Odysseus and his men are stranded on her island Aeaea, whereupon she promptly converts them into swine—a fate Odysseus himself escapes with the aid of the herb moly. Circe reconsiders and restores the hero's men, but detains them all for a year, after which she packs them off with dire tales of what they'll be up against on their way home.

CLEISTHENES (sixth century B.C.)—Athenian who conspired with Sparta to overthrow tyranny back home; founder of democracy at Athens; *see* OSTRACISM.

CREON—In Greek legend, brother of Jocasta and thus uncle and brother-in-law of Oedipus. After Oedipus unwittingly kills his father Laius, Creon takes charge of Thebes and crowns Oedipus king after the latter has solved the riddle of the Sphinx. Things get ugly when Oedipus's crime is exposed; Creon takes back the Theban crown and persecutes Oedipus's family. This tale is told in Sophocles' *Antigone* [*see* NOTHING IS MORE WONDERFUL THAN MAN].

CROESUS (sixth century B.C.)—King of Lydia after 560 B.C., and a tragi-comic figure in Herodotus's *Histories; see* pp. 43–45.

CYRUS (sixth century B.C.)—Founder of the Persian empire, who subdued Croesus and absorbed the kingdom of Lydia. His just rule became legend among the Greeks.

DAEDALUS—Legendary Greek architect and inventor, who built the original labyrinth for King Minos of Crete [*see* TO MEANDER]. Minos later turned on Daedalus, and locked him up with his son Icarus; but resourceful Daedalus constructed wings of wax by which they escaped. Icarus flew unwisely close to the sun, and plunged to his death in the Aegean.

DAMOCLES (fourth century B.C.)—Foolish courtier of Dionysius I, Tyrant of Syracuse; *see* A SWORD OF DAMOCLES.

DEMOSTHENES (383–322 B.C.)—Athenian famous for his oratorical skills; *see* TO SMELL OF THE LAMP.

DIOGENES (fourth century B.C.)—Cynic philosopher from Sinope who lived in Athens and Corinth; *see* p. 57.

DIOGENES LAERTIUS (ca. A.D. 200–250)—Diogenes, born in Cilicia, now southeastern Turkey, is virtually unknown to us outside of his one extant work, the *Lives of Eminent Philosophers*, a curious mixture of biography, anecdote, and popularized philosophy. Diogenes covers eighty-two philosophers, from Thales to Epicurus, in ten books.

DOMITIAN (Titus Flavius Domitianus; A.D. 51–96)—Roman emperor from A.D. 81, younger son of the Emperor Vespasian. A confirmed and bloody tyrant, though a considerable administrator, Domitian was murdered in A.D. 96 with the complicity of his own wife.

DRACO (seventh century B.C.)—Athenian lawmaker, now famous for the severity of his legal code; see p. 37.

ELECTRA—In Greek legend, daughter of Agamemnon and Clytaemestra, and sister of Orestes; the subject of several tragedies; see OEDIPUS COMPLEX.

EMPEDOCLES (484–424 B.C.)—Sicilian philosopher and scientist; inventor of rhetoric; see p. 69.

ENNIUS (Quintus Ennius; 239–169 B.C.)—Early Latin poet, called the "father of Roman poetry"; author of tragedies, comedies, satires, epic history, etc.

EPICURUS (341–270 B.C.)—Athenian philosopher who made pleasure his chief good; see p. 59.

ERASMUS, DESIDERIUS (A.D. 1466–1536)—A prolific and extremely influential humanist scholar from Rotterdam, Erasmus played a key role in the transmission of classical literature to Renaissance Europe. Best known for his *Praise of Folly*, Erasmus is important here for his collection of adages, which records in Latin a number of classical sayings and proverbs. Erasmus is also important for helping to establish in England and elsewhere a classical grammar-school curriculum in the early sixteenth century.

EURIPIDES (ca. 480–406 B.C.)—Greek tragic dramatist, best known for his plays *Medea* and *Bacchae; see* p. 108.

GORDIUS—A legendary figure presumed to have lived in about the eighth century B.C., Gordius was a peasant who became king of Phrygia, now northeastern Turkey. His son Midas is famous for his "golden touch." *See* A GORDIAN KNOT.

GYGES (seventh century B.C.)—A Lydian who became king by way of assassination; mentioned by Herodotus and Plato; see p. 87.

HADRIAN (Publius Aelius Hadrianus; A.D. 76–138)—Spanish-born Roman emperor, ruled from A.D. 117; known for his peaceful administration and patronage of learning and the arts.

HECTOR—Prince and greatest warrior of Troy; one of the main protagonists of Homer's *Iliad*. *See* TO HECTOR.

HECUBA—Queen of Troy, wife of Priam, mother of many children, weeping and wailing figure in Homer's *Iliad* and Shakespeare's *Hamlet*.

HELEN OF TROY—Her face, according to Christopher Marlowe, launched a thousand ships; actually a Greek, daughter of Zeus by Leda, wife of the Spartan king Menelaus. Helen was awarded to the Trojan prince Paris when he judged Aphrodite the most beautiful of goddesses; these events sparked the Trojan War [*see* p. 3].

HERODOTUS (ca. 485–425 B.C.)—First historian in the West, born at Halicarnassus, a settlement of Dorian Greeks on the coast of Asia Minor; *see* p. 32.

HESIOD (ca. eighth century B.C.)—Second of the great Greek poets, after Homer; his main surviving works are *Works and Days* and the *Theogony*. The former is an eclectic poem, mixing a first-person account of his experience as a farmer with fables and practical advice; the latter is a narrative genealogy of the Greek gods. *See* HALF IS MORE THAN THE WHOLE.

HIPPOCRATES (ca. 460–377 B.C.)—Greek physician and author of seventy-two works on medicine; *see* ART IS LONG, LIFE IS SHORT *and* THE HIPPOCRATIC OATH.

HOMER (ca. eighth century B.C.)—Greek epic poet, presumed author of the *Iliad* and *Odyssey; see* p. 1.

HORACE (Quintus Horatius Flaccus; 65–8 B.C.)—Roman poet and critic; *see* p. 143.

JASON—Famous for his quest of the Golden Fleece. According to the legend, a strange series of events brings a golden-fleeced ram to Colchis, at the east end of the Black Sea, where it is sacrificed to Zeus. The Golden Fleece itself is preserved and set under the watch of a fierce dragon. Jason, meanwhile, attempts to gain the throne of Iolcos in Thessaly, which is his by birthright but which has been usurped by his uncle Pelias. When Pelias promises to hand over rule if Jason recovers the Golden Fleece—a difficult task indeed—Jason sets out on the ship *Argo* with a crew thereby called "Argonauts." For the rest of the tale, *see* THE ARGONAUTS.

JOCASTA—Wife and, unfortunately, mother of Oedipus.

JULIUS CAESAR (Gaius Julius Caesar; 102–44 B.C.)—After holding a series of lesser political offices, and after flirting with the dangerous Catiline,

Julius Caesar had his first real taste of power as a Roman consul in 59 B.C., when he forged an alliance with Pompey and Crassus (both powerful and well-armed military leaders), now known as the "First Triumvirate." Crassus died, leaving the surviving triumvirs to ponder how well each could do without the other. With Pompey ensconced at Rome, Caesar boldly crossed the Rubicon to start a civil war [*see* p. 172]. Pompey was routed, leaving Caesar as sole dictator of Rome; but the republican spirit was still sufficiently strong to prompt a conspiracy, led by Brutus and Cassius, to assassinate Caesar in 44 B.C. [*see* ET TU, BRUTE?].

JUVENAL (ca. A.D. 60–128)—Roman satirist; *see* p. 155.

LAIUS—Legendary King of Thebes; father and victim of Oedipus.

LIVY (Titus Livius; 59 B.C.–A.D. 17)—Historian of Rome, born at Padua; *see* p. 162.

LUCAN (Marcus Annaeus Lucanus; A.D. 39–65)—Latin poet born in Spain, grandson of Seneca the Elder. Lucan made the mistake of attracting attention from the emperor Nero; *see* p. 90.

LUCIAN (born ca. A.D. 120)—Hailing from Samosata, east of the Euphrates River, Lucian was a sort of traveling rhetorician before he settled in Athens and immersed himself in ancient and modern Greek philosophies. From that point he was hooked. Though more famous today for his satires, Lucian nevertheless wrote numerous more serious dialogues, à la Plato, for example *Hermotimus*.

LUCRETIUS (Titus Lucretius Carus; 94–55 B.C.)—The principal Latin exponent of Epicurean philosophy, Lucretius is best remembered today for *De Rerum Natura* [*On the Nature of Things*], an encyclopedic poem which sets forth Epicurus's theory that the universe is composed of an infinite number of atoms. Lucretius also attempts to account for free will, the soul, the fear of death, sensual perception, and the evils of love. *See* ONE MAN'S MEAT IS ANOTHER'S POISON.

MAECENAS (Gaius Maecenas; d. 8 B.C.)—Close friend of Augustus and most famous Roman patron of the arts; financial backer of Virgil and Horace, among others; said to have inspired Virgil's *Georgics*. The poet Martial wrote, in one of his *Epigrams*, "Let there be Maecenases . . . and Virgils will not be lacking."

MARC ANTONY—see ANTONY, MARC.

MAUSOLUS (fourth century B.C.)—King of Caria, now southwestern Turkey, who inspired the MAUSOLEUM at Halicarnassus, one of the SEVEN WONDERS OF THE WORLD; *see* p. 41.

MEDEA—Princess of Colchis, niece of Circe, and enchantress in her own right. Falls in love with Jason and aids in his recovery of the Golden Fleece. She gets rather more bloody after that, cutting her brother into pieces and doing away with Jason's usurping uncle Pelias by boiling him in a cauldron. Medea and Jason flee to Corinth, where Jason is betrothed to the king's daughter; Medea, furious, kills everybody involved, except Jason himself.

MENANDER (341–290 B.C.)—Athenian comic dramatist, principal master of the "New Comedy"; *see* p. 109.

MENTOR—A character in Homer's *Odyssey;* see p. 12.

MITHRIDATES VI (131–63 B.C.)—King of Pontus, in northern Asia Minor, and a confirmed enemy of Rome. While Rome had other pressing business to attend to, Mithridates boldly seized whatever territory he could, but his expansionist designs were halted when his own son turned against him. As he was about to fall into the hands of his enemies, Mithridates ordered one of his guards to kill him (he was unable to poison himself—*see* TO TAKE WITH A GRAIN OF SALT).

NERO (Nero Claudius Caesar, born Lucius Domitius Ahenobarbus; A.D. 37–68)—Roman emperor from A.D. 54. A brutal ruler, Nero nevertheless cultivated the arts, many of which he thought himself master. (As he was about to kill himself after being abandoned by practically everybody in Rome, Nero exclaimed: "What an artist dies in me!") A few revealing facts: Nero had both his mother and wife murdered; he is said to have sung while a fire consumed Rome [*see* p. 183]; when his government and armies finally revolted against him, he planned to turn their purpose by appearing before them and weeping.

ODYSSEUS [a.k.a. ULYSSES]—King of Ithaca who appears in Homer's *Iliad* and is the chief protagonist of the *Odyssey; see* pp. 1 and 11.

OEDIPUS—Most famous Greek tragic hero, who unwittingly kills his father Laius and later marries his mother Jocasta, queen of Thebes, after solving the riddle of the Sphinx. When the terrible truth comes out, Jocasta hangs herself, Oedipus blinds himself, and he is banished. He wanders with his daughter Antigone to Colonus, where he dies of old age. *See* OEDIPUS COMPLEX.

OVID (Publius Ovidius Naso; 43 B.C.–A.D. 17?)—As a sensitive but somewhat spoiled youth, Ovid abandoned the legal career his father had hoped for him and proceeded to make quite a name for himself in Rome as a poet of the senses. Unfortunately, his poem *The Art of Love* (an adulterer's handbook) offended Caesar Augustus's sensibilities, which offense, compounded with some obscure "error" (perhaps an affair with the emperor's daughter Julia), earned him exile in A.D. 8 to Tomis—the Roman equivalent of Siberia—on the Black Sea, now Constanta in southwestern Romania. While there he wrote the personal, and rather melancholic, *Tristia* (*Sad Things*); but he is best known for the earlier *Metamorphoses*, a poem in fifteen books which collects stories of strange transformations.

PARIS [a.k.a. ALEXANDROS]—Trojan prince who would indirectly cause the destruction of Troy by Greece; *see* THE TROJAN WAR.

PARMENIDES (fifth century B.C.)—Legislator and philosopher of Elea, who propounded the theory that Being is All and All is One; mentor of Zeno of Elea [*see* ZENO'S PARADOX].

PATROCLUS—Achilles' best friend in Homer's *Iliad;* when Patroclus is slain by Hector, Achilles comes out of retirement to avenge his friend's death.

PENELOPE—In Homer's *Odyssey*, the loyal and patient wife of Odysseus. Beset by obnoxious suitors who are all convinced Odysseus is dead, Penelope puts them off until she can finish weaving a shroud for her late father-in-law (each night she unravels the day's work). The suitors are routed when Odysseus finally returns home; *see* SARDONIC.

PETRONIUS (Titus, or Gaius, Petronius Arbiter, d. A.D. 65)—A courtier of the emperor Nero, and presumed author of a now fragmentary novel, called *Satyricon*, detailing the exploits of three rather coarse but realistically drawn young men. On Petronius's career and death, *see* AN ARBITER OF TASTE.

PHAEDRUS (ca. 15 B.C.–A.D. 50)—A Macedonian who came early to Rome and then established himself as a writer of fables, many of them adaptations of Aesop's. Some of these were suspected of veiling political criticisms, which brought Phaedrus the unwanted attention of Caesar Tiberius's favorite Sejanus, who had the fabulist punished; *see* ADD INSULT TO INJURY.

PHEIDIPPIDES (fifth century B.C.)—Famous Greek long-distance runner; *see* A MARATHON.

PHILIP II OF MACEDON (ca. 382–336 B.C.)—Father of Alexander the Great; gradually brought Greece under Macedonian subjection, completing the task in 338 B.C. Philip's liaison with Cleopatra brought down the wrath of his wife Olympias, who had him assassinated. Their son Alexander, who perhaps had a hand in this deed, would finish the job by engineering the death of Philip's son by Cleopatra. A tight family.

PHOCYLIDES (sixth century B.C.)—An early Greek poet from Miletus, in Asia Minor. Phocylides is attributed with fragmentary poems, almost certainly not his own, which embody in verse the typical attitudes and moral precepts of the day. *See* THE TONGUE IS SHARPER THAN THE SWORD.

PINDAR (ca. 520–440 B.C.)—Greek lyric poet of Spartan descent; Pindar was famous even in his own time, and is remembered today chiefly for his Olympian and Pythian Odes, which celebrated individuals victorious at the Olympic and Pythian Games, respectively.

PLATO (ca. 428–348 B.C.)—Greatest of the classical Greek philosophers, author chiefly of dialogues featuring his teacher Socrates; *see* p. 83.

PLAUTUS (Titus Maccius Plautus; ca. 251–184 B.C.)—Author of brisk comedies, modeled on the Greek "New Comedy"; *see* p. 122.

PLINY THE ELDER (Gaius Plinius Secundus; A.D. 24–79)—Roman soldier, politician, and encyclopedist; *see* p. 149.

PLINY THE YOUNGER (Gaius Plinius Caecilius Secundus; ca. A.D. 61–113)— Nephew of Pliny the Elder, Roman magistrate, and Stoic. Famous for his letters, which are unspontaneous but not insincere; they cover a broad range of current topics.

PLUTARCH (ca. A.D. 46–120)—Though hardly remembered and even less read today, Plutarch was once one of the best beloved of classical authors, primarily because of his strong ethical bent. Born at Chaeronea in central Greece, Plutarch appears to have been a priest of Apollo at Delphi and a minor figure in local politics. Unhappy with the low moral caliber of the times, when Greece was part of the decaying Roman empire, Plutarch turned to Stoicism; he composed lectures and his famous biographies (the *Parallel Lives*) with an eye to revealing that the ancient greatness of Greece and Rome was predicated on moral virtue. Among many later writers, Shakespeare notably turned to Plutarch, via Sir Thomas North's 1579 translation of a French text of the *Lives*, for many of the details and even some of the language of three plays.

POMPEY (Gnaius Pompeius; 106–48 B.C.)—Great Roman general who squandered his political power. Included in the "First Triumvirate" with Julius Caesar and Crassus; but after the latter's death, Pompey unwisely provoked a civil war with Caesar, who crushed him.

PROPERTIUS (Sextus Propertius; b. ca. 50 B.C.)—A Roman love poet who based his work on Greek lyricism. Many poems are addressed to the pseudonymous "Cynthia" (compare Catullus's "Lesbia"), who caused the poet as much pain as pleasure, and thus much of his writing is melancholic. Ezra Pound paints a fine portrait of Propertius and his times in "Homage to Sextus Propertius" (1917).

PYRRHON OF ELIS (ca. 360–270 B.C.)—Greek painter and later philosopher, founder of Skepticism; see p. 74.

PYRRHUS (319–272 B.C.)—Second cousin of Alexander the Great and king of Epirus (now northwestern Greece and southern Albania) after 307 B.C.; see A PYRRHIC VICTORY.

PYTHAGORAS (ca. 572–500 B.C.)—Greek philosopher and mathematician, familiar with Egyptian metaphysics, who established an ascetic brotherhood that later ran into trouble because of its undemocratic political doctrines. Pythagoras claimed to have been inspired by Apollo (his name means something like "Delphic spokesman"), who perhaps taught him about right triangles and the mathematical basis of musical tones, as well as informing him that the earth is round. See THE TRANSMIGRATION OF SOULS.

QUINTILIAN (Marcus Fabius Quintilianus; ca. A.D. 35–95)—Latin rhetorician and tutor, author of the exhaustive *Institutes of Oratory,* which, despite its tedium, proved massively influential in the Renaissance revival of classical literature and rhetoric.

ROMULUS AND REMUS—Legendary twins and founders of Rome; see p. 164.

SAPPHO (b. ca. 612 B.C.)—Poet who lived on the island of Lesbos, but who was forced to retire to Sicily because of political troubles; see LESBIAN.

SEJANUS (Lucius Aelius Sejanus; d. A.D. 31)—Vile right-hand man of Tiberius Caesar. Incorrigibly power-hungry, he perhaps had a hand in the poisoning of Tiberius's son Drusus. Though for a time, when Tiberius had retired (as it was thought) to debauch himself at an island retreat, Sejanus was Rome's leading man, his plots became so obvious that even the emperor was no longer fooled; Tiberius wrote a long letter to the senate denouncing Sejanus, who was then put to death. The alienated masses tore his corpse to shreds.

SENECA THE ELDER (Lucius, or Marcus Annaeus, Seneca; ca. 55 B.C.–A.D. 40)—Roman rhetorician of Spanish origin, famed for his astounding memory.

SENECA THE YOUNGER (Lucius Annaeus Seneca; ca. 5 B.C.–A.D. 65)—Son of Seneca the Elder; Roman senator in the time of Caligula, which proved to be a dangerous occupation. Seneca was forced to retire to Corsica in A.D. 41, but later returned to Rome as Nero's tutor [see TO LIVE ACCORDING TO NATURE]. Seneca wrote on every imaginable topic, but is best remembered for his dialogues, moral epistles, and histrionic tragedies.

THE SEVEN SAGES OF GREECE (sixth century B.C.)—Thales of Miletus, Pittacus of Mytilene, Bias of Priene, Solon of Athens, Cleobulus of Lindus, Myson of Chen (or Periander or Anacharsis), and Chilon of Sparta; *see* p. 72.

SOCRATES (469–399 B.C.)—Socrates of Athens seems to have been an almost superhuman figure, possessed of extraordinary moral courage and physical strength, distinguished in battle, politically incorruptible, brilliant and witty. He is also said to have been rather ugly, and his wife Xantippe later became legendary as a shrew. It also seems that early in his life he distinguished himself in physical science, but later turned to ethics after the Oracle at Delphi pronounced that no one was wiser than Socrates. He became famous for the "Socratic method" of moral instruction, in which he led his audience to the proper conclusions by posing questions. If he had any particular philosophical program, it is now inextricable from the one Plato attributes to him in a series of brilliant dialogues; but it is doubtful the Plato's Socrates accurately reflects the beliefs of the historical figure. Socrates was condemned to die in 399 B.C. when a jury found him guilty of religious perversity and of corrupting the minds of Athens' youth [*see* A CUP OF HEMLOCK].

SOLON (ca. 640–560 B.C.)—Statesman and poet; reformer of the Athenian constitution. Solon helped establish true democracy in Athens by putting an end to serfdom, opening political office to a broader range of citizens, and establishing a more just legal system.

SOPHOCLES (ca. 496–406 B.C.)—Born at Colonus, the setting of his tragedy *Oedipus at Colonus*, Sophocles has generally been regarded as the greatest classical author of tragic drama. Of his 120 plays, seven survive; *see* p. 108.

STATIUS (Publius Papinius Statius; ca. A.D. 45–96)—Though all but forgotten today, Statius, a Neapolitan, was regarded in the Middle Ages and Renaissance as one of the greatest classical poets; he occupies a place of pride in Dante's *Divine Comedy*. He was popular in his own day as well, and counted the emperor Domitian among his admirers. His principal works include the *Thebias*, which adds details to the Oedipus story, and the *Achilleis*, which recounts the early career of the hero Achilles.

STENTOR—Greek herald, a character in Homer's *Iliad*; see STENTORIAN.

STRABO (ca. 64 B.C.–A.D. 21)—Stoic Greek geographer and historian; his *Geography* accounts for the physical makeup, history, and customs of countries ranging from India and Egypt to Britain.

SUETONIUS (Gaius Suetonius Tranquillus; ca. A.D. 69–140)—A lawyer and later a failure as a politician under the emperor Hadrian, Suetonius is remembered chiefly for his historical biographies of the first twelve Caesars, from Julius to Domitian. Also surviving are some of his biographies of Roman authors.

TACITUS (Cornelius Tacitus; ca. A.D. 55–118)—One of the greatest classical historians; see p. 162.

TEIRESIAS—Blind soothsayer of Thebes; his ghost appears in Homer's *Odyssey* (Book 10), and alive he plays a leading role in the downfall of Oedipus [*see* THE RIDDLE OF THE SPHINX]. Teiresias is in Greek legend a figure of ambiguous sexual identity, and one whose blindness is variously related to forbidden sexual knowledge. In one account, he is blinded after seeing Athena bathing. In another, after gaining the power to change sex by striking a pair of copulating snakes with his staff, he is charged by Zeus and Hera with deciding whether men or women enjoy sex more; when he answers that women do, Hera, enraged, blinds him, but then Zeus grants him nearly divine foresight.

TELEMACHUS—Son of Odysseus in Homer's *Odyssey*.

TERENCE (Publius Terentius Afer; ca. 195–159 B.C.)—Most sophisticated Roman author of comic drama; *see* p. 122.

THALES (b. ca. 624 B.C.)—One of the Seven Sages of Greece; believed that water was the primary element; is said to have invented geometry; *see* p. 53.

THEOPHRASTUS (ca. 372–288 B.C.)—Student of Aristotle; crucial to the development of the Peripatetic school of philosophy; insanely prolific author; best-remembered for his brief character sketches.

THESPIS (sixth century B.C.)—Early Greek tragedian; *see* THESPIAN.

THRASO—The braggart soldier of Terence's comedy *The Eunuch; see* THRASONICAL.

THUCYDIDES (ca. 455–400 B.C.)—The greatest Greek historian; wrote tersely and objectively of the Peloponnesian War (431–404 B.C.) between coalitions led by Athens and Sparta [*see* p. 48]. Exiled from Athens after a military failure, Thucydides was readmitted twenty years later; he is said to have been assassinated within four years.

TIBERIUS (Tiberius Claudius Nero Caesar; 42 B.C.–A.D. 37)—Emperor of Rome after A.D. 14, stepson and successor of Augustus. A military genius, Tiberius turned out to be an unpopular emperor, despite his efficient and generally just administration. In old age he retired to Capri, an island off Naples, where he was thought to pass his time in debauchery and decadence; though probably untrue, the rumors only encouraged the appalling political and moral decline back in Rome, a decline Tiberius proved powerless to check.

TROILUS—Trojan prince with a minor role in Homer's *Iliad*; best remembered as a character in works by Boccaccio, Chaucer, and Shakespeare.

VESPASIAN (Titus Flavius Vespasianus; A.D. 9–79)—Roman emperor from A.D. 69, succeeding Nero. Vespasian is noteworthy for having effectively cleaned up the mess left by his predecessor; his reign was peaceful and marked by a revival in public works and the arts. *See* MONEY DOESN'T SMELL.

VESTAL VIRGIN—Generic name for attendants of the fire at the Roman Temple of Vesta, goddess of the hearth. The temple was associated with the king's household in the times before the Roman Republic. The Vestals, four or six in number, were severely punished—by being buried or burned alive—if they violated their vow of chastity; *see* ROMULUS AND REMUS.

VIRGIL (Publius Vergilius Maro; 70–19 B.C.)—Greatest Latin poet; author of the *Aeneid; see* p. 138.

XENOPHANES (sixth century B.C.)—Greek poet and philosopher with unorthodox, monotheistic beliefs; *see* NOTHING COMES FROM NOTHING.

XERXES (fifth century B.C.)—King of Persia after 485 B.C.; in 480, Xerxes launched an invasion of Greece, but was humiliated by forces under Athenian command.

ZENO OF CITIUM (335–263 B.C.)—Academic philosopher and founder of the Stoic school; *see* STOIC.

ZENO OF ELEA (b. ca. 490 B.C.)—Student of Parmenides who advanced his teacher's philosophy by means of paradoxes; *see* ZENO'S PARADOX.

About the Translations

Unless otherwise indicated, all translations from Latin are my own, based largely on the texts supplied by the Loeb Classical Library, now published by Harvard University Press. I have frequently used the Loeb translations as a reference. Translations from Italian and French are also mine. Otherwise, I have relied wholly or in part on the following translations:

AESOP: various hands.

ARISTOPHANES: Anonymous (London, 1912).

ARISTOTLE, *Poetics* and *Rhetoric:* Thomas Taylor (London, 1811); *Politics:* Benjamin Jowett (Oxford, 1885); *On the Heavens:* the French of Paul Moraux (Paris, 1965); *Physics:* Philip H. Wicksteed and F. M. Cornford (Loeb translation).

ARRIAN: Edward James Chinnock (London, 1893); E. Iliff Robson (Loeb translation).

THE BIBLE: King James Version (London, 1611).

DIOGENES LAERTIUS: the French translation by Robert Genaille (Paris, 1965).

EMPEDOCLES: the French translation by Jean Zafiropulo (Paris, 1953).

EPICURUS: the French translation by Jean Bollack et al. (Paris, 1971); Cyril Bailey (Oxford, 1926).

EURIPIDES: various hands.

HERODOTUS: George Rawlinson (New York, 1860); Aubrey de Sélincourt (Harmondsworth, 1954).

HESIOD: Thomas Cooke (London, 1728); Charles Abraham Elton (London, 1812).

HIPPOCRATES: Francis Adams (New York, 1886); W. H. S. Jones (Loeb translation).

HOMER: George Chapman (London, 1598–1614); *Odyssey* 20.299–303: Thomas Hobbes (London, 1674–5).

LUCIAN, *Demonax:* H. W. and F. G. Fowler (Oxford, 1905); *Hermotimus:* Augusta M. Campbell Davidson (London, 1902).

MENANDER: Francis G. Allinson (Loeb translation).

PETRONIUS: Oscar Wilde [attrib.] (before 1900; repr. New York, 1930).

PHOCYLIDES: the French rendering by Pascale Derron (Paris, 1986).

PLATO: Benjamin Jowett (Oxford, 1871).

PLUTARCH: Sir Thomas North (London, 1579), except *Maxims of the Philosophers*: John Dowel, and "The Impossibility of Pleasure according to Epicurus": William Baxter (New York, 1859).

SOPHOCLES: the French translation by Robert Pignarre (Paris, 1947).

STRABO: W. Falconer (London, 1889).

SUETONIUS: Philemon Holland (London, 1606).

THUCYDIDES: Benjamin Jowett (Oxford, 1881).

Index

Ascham, Roger, 19
Asclepius, 64
Athena, 3, 12, 13, 37, 208, 211, 224
Atomism, 198
Auden, W. H., 117
August, 191
Augustus, 58, 138, 143, 150, 167, 170, 179, 181, 191, 213, 218, 225
Aventine, 166

Bacon, Francis, 50, 78
Baldwin, William, 145
Barker, E. Phillips, 67
Barnfield, Richard, 133
Beg the question, 202
Bellerophon, 8–9, 213–214
Bentham, Jeremy, 63
Better never to have been born, 117
Beware of Greeks bearing gifts, 14
Beware the Ides of March, 177
Bias of Priene, 72
Bible, 130, 136; Book of Jeremiah, 30; I Corinthians, 202; Ecclesiastes, 129; Gospel According to Luke, 207; Gospel According to Matthew, 31, 208; Isaiah, 18
Bion of Borysthenes, 208
Bite the dust, 5
Blow hot and cold, 24
Boccaccio, Giovanni, 225
Bread and circuses, 156
Brontë, Charlotte, 173
Brown, John, 57
Brutus, Marcus, 143, 177, 178, 180–181, 203, 213, 218
Bulwer-Lytton, Edward George, 200
Burke, Edmund, 28
Burton, Robert, 29
Bush, George, 103
Butler, Samuel, 179
Byron, George Gordon, Lord, 127

Cabbalism, 80
Caelian, 167
Caesar, 170—see also Julius Caesar
Caesar salad, 170
Caesarean section, 171
Calendar, 189–191
Caligula, 191, 222
Call a spade a spade, 120
Call no man happy until he dies, 43–44
Callippus, 84
Canary, 150
Capitoline, 166
Cardini, Caesar, 170
Carlyle, Thomas, 66, 96, 186
Carpe diem, 148
Carthago delenda est, 214
Cassius, Gaius, 177, 180–181, 213, 218
Cast out nature with a fork, it will still return/If you, 144
Catiline, 131, 214, 217
Cato of Utica, 180–181, 203, 214
Cato the Censor, 162, 179, 214
Catullus, 206, 214, 221
Caveat emptor, 206
Central Park, 144
Chapman, George, 7, 208
Chaucer, Geoffrey, 96, 140, 142, 152, 155, 179, 199, 201, 205, 206, 225
Chesterfield, Lord, 12
Chilon, 72, 77, 102, 145, 214
Chimera, 9, 213, 214
Cicero, 96, 120, 131, 188, 204, 214; *Laws*, 136; *Letters to His Friends*, 132, 207; *Of Duties*, 205; *Of Friendship*, 133; *Of the Orator*, 137; *Tusculan Disputations*, 134, 135
Circe, 16, 18, 20, 215, 219
Circus Maximus, 161
Claudius, 191
Cleisthenes, 47, 215
Cleobulus of Lindus, 72, 145
Cleopatra, 211, 212, 220

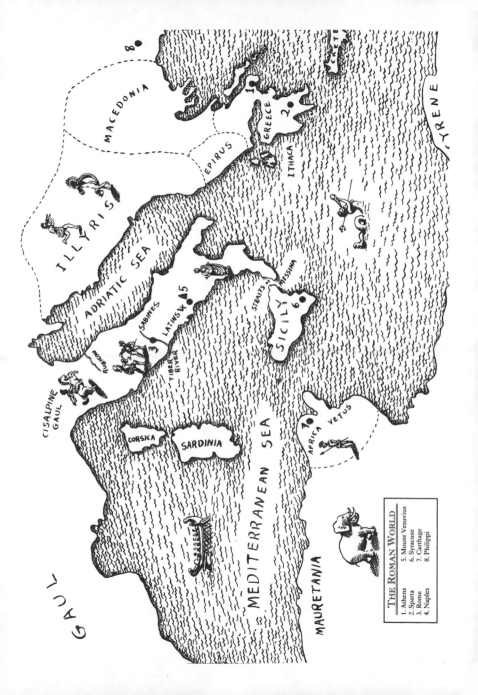

THE ROMAN WORLD
1. Athens
2. Sparta
3. Rome
4. Naples
5. Mount Vesuvius
6. Syracuse
7. Carthage
8. Philippi